# Fueled by Misery

## My journey through life with Muscular Dystrophy

### By Peter Li

Learn more about this book
and its author by visiting our web site:
www.overboardministries.com

*This work depicts actual events in the life of the author as truthfully as recollection permits and/or can be verified by research. Occasionally, dialogue consistent with the character or nature of the person speaking has been supplemented. All persons within are actual individuals; there are no composite characters. The names of some individuals have been changed to respect their privacy.*

# Dedication

This book is dedicated to my mom, Lily, the strongest person I know. She is always there and never gives up caring for me through the good and bad times.

I would like to thank David Erickson,
my best friend, for showing me life beyond MD;

Carole Haes Landon,
for pushing me to finish this book of mine;

and my brother, Jason,
for putting up with me.

# CONTENTS

# Preface

My name is Peter Li, and I have Becker's Muscular Dystrophy (BMD). The reason I am telling you this is that I want to share my life story with as many people as I can. By giving the world a glimpse of my inner self, I am trying to change at least one person's heart.

All the things you're going to read about are what I feel deep down inside, and while you can expect a lot of pain as you read about my life struggles, you will also experience times of great joy. I'm telling you this now because if you meet me in person you wouldn't suspect that I'm upset or angry at MD. I don't act as if I am down. I'm always laughing and joking about life. Because of this, I feel no one really understands what it is like to be me. Perhaps they would if they were somehow given the opportunity to spend a day in my shoes. That can't happen, though, so the only way I can let people know what MD is like is by writing about my life experiences and emotions related to the disorder. I realize this is not the same as having MD because some things can't be expressed through words. Furthermore, this is a different kind of story because most people in my situation have a difficult time opening their hearts and sharing their feelings with strangers. They keep quiet because they feel uncomfortable talking about personal things. I, on the other hand, feel this is an important opportunity to let everyone experience the emotional side of MD.

Up until now, even my family has been in the dark. They couldn't tell if I was depressed or not. Yet there have been times where everything brought me down. In spite of this, I would have never allowed my mom to know this. I felt I had to be strong for her. If I hadn't, she would have been upset and blamed herself for my sadness. That isn't acceptable to me.

I realize it is going to be difficult to write these things, but I feel I have something to offer and keeping my emotions inside does no one any good. It hurts so much feeling the way I do about everything around me. I would cry about it, but I can't cry anymore. I finished with that a long time ago. All I ask is that you keep an open mind when you read this and please don't feel sorry for me. I don't like it when people do that.

Peter Li

# 1. My Family

I was born in Tung Nghia, Lâm Đ`ông, Vietnam, and immigrated to the United States when I was about six months old, in June of 1979. I'm not Vietnamese; I'm Chinese. I can still speak my native language. My family speaks Cantonese, the simplified form.

**Wavering Fate**

After America left the Vietnam War, my family wanted to leave the country because Vietnam became Communist. They wanted freedom.

We had to pay the government in gold to be able to leave the country and to build boats. We didn't have any. My great-uncles #2, #3, #5, #6, and #7 paid for us. My family and relatives built a boat and wanted to go to America. We didn't even know where America was, and yet we still set sail.

There were 448 people packed onto a small boat. No room to move around. Many of my relatives were with us (my dad, mom, sister, and me; I was 6 months old).

While out on the sea, ten to eleven boats came circling around our boat. They were Thai pirates. They had their guns drawn. Our boat stopped out of fear. Everyone was scared. Mothers were holding their children tight. The pirates demanded anything of value: gold pieces, gold teeth, jewelry, and young girls to sell or whatever. They took everything. My mom, Lily Li, was frantic because she didn't know who had my sister. She thought one of my relatives had her. My dad, David Li, was holding my sister tightly. He didn't allow anyone to hold her. My mom held onto me.

Then an American battleship, the USS Robert E. Peary, came and the pirates scattered and fled away. We were saved. The crew gave us medical help, food, and water. All 448 of us boarded the ship. (Do) We were relieved that we didn't have to be stranded in the ocean anymore. There wasn't enough food to go around. We went to Thailand to wait for the paperwork to be done for instant U.S. citizenship. We were there for a month.

We had our pictures taken so that maybe someone would sponsor us. And we were sponsored by a couple, Melvin and Lilly Larin, from Anaheim, California, a very nice couple who took my family in. When our paperwork was done, we went to Japan for one night. Then we were flown to LAX. We arrived in America finally.

My immediate family consists of seven members. We've lived in Norco, California, since the year 2000. I have one sister and three younger brothers. My siblings and I are roughly a year apart. My oldest sibling is my sister, Anh. I'm the second oldest. My brother Steven is the middle child. The next youngest is Jason. Jason and I both have MD. Finally, there's my youngest brother, Jimmy.

My family is typical of most Asian families. My siblings and I don't talk much to each other. We're all doing our own thing. My family does spend quality time together though. We always have dinner as a family, even though there isn't much conversation. We are supposed to eat quietly, so we can finish quickly. It is typical for Asian families to keep their emotions hidden. We don't give hugs or share our affections with one another, even when we're sad. We're taught not to show weakness.

We do get together with my immediate relatives. The entire Ly family has grown too large to keep in touch with. It would be impossible to keep up with everyone's names and which side of the family they're on. Who are cousins? Who are aunts and uncles? Besides, during the emigration process, some kept the original last name of "Ly." Some changed it to "Lee." My family changed our last name to "Li."

# 2. Muscular Dystrophy

The physical aspects of MD are just a small part of the overall hardships of living with MD. The emotional aspects of MD are the hardest to deal with. The real struggle with MD lies within the heart. It determines whether MD will win, or you will win over MD in spite of the deteriorating physical aspects. Only the emotional aspects of MD can be modified.

**Muscular Dystrophy (MD)**

There are many types of muscular dystrophies (MD), but I'll name the two that relate to me. Muscular dystrophies are progressive muscle disorders that cause muscle wasting and weakness on a cellular level. As time goes by, the muscle cells deteriorate slowly, causing loss of strength.

**Duchenne's Muscular Dystrophy (DMD)**

From the Muscular Dystrophy Association website, DMD was first discovered and named by a French neurologist, Guillaume-Benjamin-Amand Duchenne, in the 1860s. DMD begins showing at an early age, around three years old. It affects the voluntary muscles: *"arms, legs, and trunk gradually weaken, and by their early teens or even earlier, the involuntary muscles, heart and respiratory muscles may be affected as well."* (Facts About Duchenne and Becker Muscular Dystrophies (DMD and BMD))

The progressiveness of DMD is predictable by physical observation. Children with this mutation often learn how to walk later than normal. Parents may notice their children's calf muscles are *"enlarged or have pseudohypertrophy."* By their preschool years, walking becomes difficult. They tend to be clumsy and fall frequently because balance becomes unstable. As time goes on, climbing stairs, getting up from the floor or running becomes difficult as well.

Almost all DMD individuals require the use of a wheelchair starting somewhere in between the ages of seven and twelve. In their teenage years, activities that involve the use of their arms, legs or trunk requires help from others or some sort of mechanical support.

**Becker's Muscular Dystrophy (BMD)**

By the 1950s, BMD was first described as a variant of DMD by a German doctor, Peter Emil Becker. BMD is very similar to DMD, but it's a *"much milder version of DMD."* BMD patients usually start showing muscle weaknesses during their teens or early adulthood, but it is *"slower and far less predictable."* Muscle deterioration *"usually begins with the hips and pelvic area, the thighs and the shoulders."* The use of wheelchairs varies from person to person; some with BMD don't require the use of a wheelchair, but require some assistance like the use of canes.

## Diagnosis

Doctors can easily get a preliminary diagnosis for DMD by performing a physical examination and getting a family history. This does not require any complicated tests. Nevertheless, there are many forms of MD and while these initial tests go a long way in directing the physician toward the disorder, other tests may be required to accurately diagnose which form of MD a child has. For example, BMD is often misdiagnosed. Therefore, further tests may include an *"electromyography or nerve conduction study"* which tests the muscle and the nerves with electrical shocks to measure whether the muscle weakness occurs in the muscle itself or the nerves. Another test that is sometimes used is called a CK level blood test or *"creatine kinase test, which measures an enzyme that leaks out of damaged muscle."* An abnormal amount of CK leakage determines that the muscle is being destroyed by MD or by an inflammation. The higher the amount of CK present the more likely the child has a form of MD, yet this doesn't determine which kind of disorder it is. A positive on this test may lead to a muscle biopsy, which is surgically removing a muscle sample to accurately determine which disorder it is. The results of the biopsy can determine either the amount of dystrophin causing BMD or the lack of dystrophin which causes DMD in the muscle cell.

## The Cause

In 1987, researchers identified DMD as caused by a mutation in a flawed gene on the X chromosome. The mutation is caused when *"a particular gene on the X chromosome fails to make the protein dystrophin."* BMD is caused by *"different mutations in the same gene."* In BMD, the mutation produces some dystrophin, but is inadequate to prevent the mutation. Even with a small amount of dystrophin, the muscle is protected from *"degenerating as badly or as quickly"* as DMD.

## Heredity

DMD and BMD are both inherited on the X chromosome, which is where the mutation occurs. Males inherit an *"X chromosome from the mother and a Y chromosome from the father, while females inherit two X chromosomes,"* one each from both mother and father. (Does It Run in the Family?)

A female with a dystrophin mutation on one of her two X chromosomes inherited by her mother doesn't produce DMD or BMD because of the other X chromosome she inherited from her father, which is a healthy dystrophin gene. The healthy gene *"gives enough of the protein to protect her from the disease,"* but she becomes a carrier of the mutation. Her sons have a *"fifty percent chance of inheriting the mutated gene,"* thus having DMD or BMD, and her daughters also have a *"fifty percent chance of inheriting the mutation and becoming a carrier."* Deciding whether or not to have children is a burden that female carriers have for the rest of their lives. Males inherit DMD or BMD because they don't have an extra X chromosome, a healthy dystrophin gene, to protect from the flawed gene. Males that have DMD or BMD *"can't pass the flawed gene to their sons,"* because males give a Y chromosome instead of an X chromosome. On the other hand, a male can pass DMD or BMD to their daughters because of the X chromosome they give. Their daughters become carriers of the mutated gene, and *"their sons will have a 50 percent chance of developing the disease, and so on."* (Does It Run in the Family?)

There are no known cures to stop or reverse DMD and BMD, and *"eating food with protein can't replace lost dystrophin."* The muscle degeneration can only be slowed down by light exercise, some medications, and stretching.

## Beginning

Life started off grand. I did everything normally: jumping, walking, basically what every other kid was doing without any difficulties. Playing with other kids was fun because I wasn't having that much difficulty walking. I couldn't run though. When I was small, my brothers and I always had to help out at the farm where my grandpa worked. It was a family business. Every summer we had to watch the birds, so they didn't eat up the recently planted seeds in the field. Scarecrows didn't work, so they set up a type of bell made with a tin box with a long string attached to it. It was boring doing that, but in a way it was fun because we were outside instead of inside. My cousins were there too because their farm was next to ours, so we always hung out together because they had to do the same thing. The bad part was that it was hot sitting out there for hours and hours. Sometimes we had to water the vegetables around four or five in the evening. It was fun spending the summer at the farm, and when it got too hot, we'd turn on the sprinklers and run through to cool off.

At the age of seven, everything began to change. I started to fall often and had difficulty getting up. I didn't know what was wrong with me, neither did my parents. Nevertheless, it was two years before my parents took me to see a doctor. I went to see Dr. Clark at Loma Linda University Medical Center. I was about nine years old. Walking to the doctor's office was tough. I remembered that I fell before I got there. I just lost my balance. I wanted to cry, not because of the physical pain; I just didn't want to make life worse for my mom, so the tears poured out. I didn't want to get up. I just sat there shaking my head, but I had to move; I couldn't just sit there all day. I dreaded finding out what was wrong with me, but I did it anyway. I found the courage from deep within.

Dr. Clark explained that I had Becker's Muscular Dystrophy (BMD). I have been his patient since that fateful day, more than half my life. He tried to explain my condition to my parents, but they couldn't comprehend all the facts; neither could I. I saw my mom crying. That's what moms feel when there's something wrong with their kids: an overwhelming sadness. Seeing my mom in tears made me realize that having MD was going to be tougher on her than me. I now knew why I was falling all the time; why getting out of bed was difficult; and from then on, my childhood disappeared.

I went to Val Verde Elementary; it's in Perris, California. I remember sitting and watching the other students playing sports during PE. During that time, I sat by myself on the swings. My friends and I always played kick ball or kick the ball in the air and catch it, but I could never catch the ball. When they kicked the ball it went pretty high, but when I kicked the ball it floundered. One day, I caught the ball for the first time, and everybody was so happy and proud of me. They all cheered.

When it was windy at school, the wind would usually blow me down or make me walk slower than usual like I was in slow motion. It was kind of funny. I went to school on those days even when my mom said not to go.

After my parents found out about my condition, we didn't go out as a family much anymore. However, when I was in the sixth grade, we did take a family trip to Las Vegas. This was the only family trip I can remember after my diagnosis. In Las Vegas, it was difficult for them to get around and see the sights because they had to wait on me. I lumbered along, so we couldn't do that much. Mostly, we rode around in the car.

My parents did take me to see my relatives. I saw my cousins often. Most of my family knew I had MD, but couldn't understand how it affected us. Often in Chinese families, disabled family members are not taken out or allowed to participate in large family functions.

My mom said, "If I knew that you were going have MD, I wouldn't have wanted to have kids." I don't blame her for saying that. She wouldn't have known about it back then (in Vietnam), because they couldn't test someone for it. I kept telling her that it wasn't her fault. She couldn't have known that I was going to have MD. Even so, in her heart she didn't believe it.

# 3. School Years

## Middle School

Later on, my parents decided to move to Lakeside, California, which is somewhere near San Diego. Because of this, I lost all my elementary school friends and had to make new ones. Luckily making friends had always come easy for me, so I didn't worry about it much. I attended Tierra Del Sol Middle School.

At the age of twelve, I had to grow up quickly. I didn't get that chance to grow up and mature slowly like everyone else. I didn't really have a childhood. At home, my parents didn't speak much English so I had to help them understand all my medical stuff, doctor visits and the decision-making process.

Walking became very difficult for me. It was very frustrating trying not to lose my balance and yet, unlike most MD patients, I never had to wear leg braces for support. I just had to be cautious of every step I took. Most of the time, I'd just lose my balance and fall. My friends and family had to be cautious when going anywhere with me. They never walked beside me because they didn't want to accidentally knock me over. They were gracious and always gave me space. When I did fall, getting up was so hard and frustrating because I couldn't just stand up like everyone else.

It was like that each day. If I was lucky, I would only fall once or twice. One time, I fell and couldn't handle it anymore, so I just sat there. I broke down and started to cry. I kept asking myself, "Why does this have to happen to me?" I kept shaking my head. Several friends walked by and saw me and asked me what had happened, but I didn't want to say anything. They sat there with me and tried to cheer me up, but I didn't want to listen. They knew what was happening with me. It was hard for them as well because they didn't know what to do to cheer me up. I just didn't want to get up anymore. It wasn't the physical pain, but the emotional pain of always losing my balance.

I didn't worry as much afterwards because my friends were always there to help me up when I fell. Despite this, I always ruined my pants and there would be a big crowd surrounding me. Then the teachers would come rushing up to see what was happening. *It was just me falling again.* It was okay though; I'd learned to go with the flow and I had my circle of friends protecting me.

I was given a choice about getting out of each class early, that way I wouldn't have to walk in a crowd of students. I often decided to do that, but I wondered: if I lost my balance and fell, who would help me up? That was always on my mind. If that happened, I would have to wait until my friends got out of class. I also got to go out earlier than everyone else to beat the crowd of students getting their lunches. At lunchtime, I sat by myself all the time because I couldn't sit with any of my friends; they were up in the bleachers. I always wondered what it was like to hang around a crowd of friends and join in their conversations.

I don't know how I developed so many connections with the other students. It could have been because I had a totally different class schedule than my classmates did because of my adapted P.E. class. In addition, my Language Arts class combined three different classes in one (Reading, Writing, and English). While everyone else had those classes consecutively in the morning, I had two in the morning and one after lunch.

After lunch, I had that one class (Reading) that I should have had in the morning, so there was a new set of students to make friends with. Then my next class was adapted P.E. My teacher was Laine McCobb. He had other kids to teach at other schools, so I had to have adaptive P.E. with the eighth graders, even though I was a sixth grader. I did what I could in the activities he had us do.

We did different sports. Laine McCobb's lessons involved learning the rules, but I already knew the rules. He didn't want me to answer all his questions. He wanted the other kids to try. I never had to do the written part of P.E. He always made me correct papers instead. We had some able-bodied students help out with the class. That was nice of them. All the other kids (besides me) in our adapted P.E. class had special education classes. I was the only Adapted P.E. student in regular education classes. As far as the class went, all the kids always wanted to play bowling for some reason. We didn't actually bowl. We had a ramp to put the bowling ball on, so all we had to do was aim and push the ball off the ramp.

Adapted P.E. was the class I enjoyed the most, because everyone was disabled. We were equals in a sense. Being in that class put my disability in the back of my mind. I was pretty much a "normal" kid during that short period of time.

One day in seventh grade, a bully made fun of the way I was walking. He told his friends. They would imitate my way of walking. They even said that I walked like a girl. I had no choice but to walk up on my toes because that was the only way I could keep my balance.

I got so upset that I told one of my friends about it, and he got furious. He happened to be the most popular person at school and he told others about it. The situation got out of control. It was bad because a crowd of people wanted to kick the bully's butt and someone ended up punching him. After a week, the bully and I had a little talk about what happened and he apologized. I accepted. I talked to my friends about it and everything got back to normal. I learned from that mistake. I shouldn't have let him bother me as much as he did.

By eighth grade, walking was extremely difficult—not just bad, but horrendous. I was constantly falling because my ankles had become so tight. I made it through the first week by holding onto a friend's shoulder when walking to my classes. By the end of the first week, I'd had enough. Every step I took I fell. Since I didn't have a wheelchair yet, I had home study and a teacher came out to the house to give me my homework. I missed half of the school year until I borrowed a manual wheelchair and I could finally go back to school.

It was so frustrating going back to school in a wheelchair. Everyone looked at me differently. They always stared. I was walking one day, and then MD took away my ability to walk, just like that. I didn't like being in a wheelchair—*who would?*— but I was also relieved. I didn't have to put up with the falling. I was able to get around more easily. Yet it could be frustrating because I had to depend on someone to push me around. Did I miss walking? Honestly, I don't miss it.

**Impact**

Everything hit me all at once, emotionally. By that I mean, I came to a self-realization about all the things I wouldn't get to do and wouldn't get to experience for myself. I could see my independent life disappearing. I still hung out with my friends, but only at school. They always took me to the basketball courts during lunch. It was so difficult being out there. I don't think any of my friends knew how hard it was for me. All I got to do was watch them play. Everywhere I looked, everyone else was having fun, doing what they wanted to do. There was another boy in a wheelchair. He was in the last stages of MD, so I could see right before my eyes how I was going to end up, severely physically disabled.

One day the principal came up to me to see how I was doing. He knew that I was frustrated because I couldn't play with my friends. He tried to cheer me up, but it didn't work. I gave up on sports after that. I don't even watch them. When everyone watches games, I go do something else. It's hard for me to understand why people make such a big deal about the Super Bowl, World Series or the NBA Finals.

One day, I was asked to join a field trip to Disneyland. Before I had the wheelchair, it would have been difficult or impossible to go to Disneyland. It was hard to get around because it was so packed with people. This time was different; I had a good time because I still had plenty of strength left. I got on every ride. I went on most of them about five times each. Then one of my friends wanted me to go to Magic Mountain with them, and I said, "Okay." The teacher said it was okay because I'd had him as a teacher before. The bus had room for me and my wheelchair (the chair was stored underneath). After we arrived at Magic Mountain, I didn't want to choose which friends would go with me, so I kept quiet (anyone that went with me could get on the rides faster). It was strange to watch my friends fight over me.

Another time I went with my friends to the bowling alley. I didn't bowl because the ball was too heavy, and I would have fallen over if I tried. I just watched them play. It was a fortunate day for me though because I got to meet one of my friend's mom (Shana Torp). She was very kind. We ended up being good friends, and she became a second mom to me.

Even though I got to do all those things, emotionally I still felt drained because I couldn't do what everyone else was doing (mainly walking and other physical activities.). When I went to the beach with the class, I didn't get to do anything except watch everyone else have fun. I didn't get to go in the sand or go into the water because I couldn't get there. I just sat in my wheelchair on the sidewalk or on the pier. I didn't watch the girls either because my mind was spinning. I was miserable. All of my friends were playing volleyball. They wanted me to get into the game, but I didn't want to. They had no idea how I was feeling. Despite my sadness, being with my friends was a respite from everyday life and I did want to stay with them as long as possible. They had room on the regular bus for me, but they couldn't put the wheelchair in, so I had to go back earlier than them. The school had to return the "special" bus at a certain time. I thought, *Oh well, at least I got to go.*

Going to the last eighth grade dance was difficult, but I went anyway. I knew what I'd face there. I just wanted to hang out with my friends one last time (ninth grade would be a new experience called High School). After the dance, everyone else got to go out for food, movies or other fun stuff, and I got to go home. I wasn't invited to any of the after-party fun. This was very difficult for me to handle. They had fun; I just went to bed. *Who's invisible? I am.*

## High School

After eighth grade, my family moved to Chino, California. We lived by dairy farms. No matter which way I turned my head, there was a dairy. It smelled all the time (cow manure everywhere), but I got used to it. It was scary living in our house. It was located between two dairies and set far off the road. It was so dark at night. I was scared rolling around in the house at night. On the good side, it was a huge house with pecan trees, so we always had pecans to eat.

My mom started taking me to see other doctors who studied Eastern medicine. They always ended up giving me prescriptions for herbal remedies, not medicine you see in the U.S. These concoctions are natural, not pills. They had to be boiled, and I had to drink a bowl of it every night. It had a nasty taste and every time I drank it I wanted to vomit. I knew what was in it as well. That was the worst part. There were a few roots, dried up bees; I think there was a crow's foot, and some kind of wood. It tasted like dirt. The whole house would reek of these things.

I didn't refuse to go to these "doctors" because if I did, it would make it harder for my mom. If seeing a doctor like that gave my mom hope that it might work for me, then I'd keep going as long as she wanted me to. I did tell her, "It's not going to work." Maybe I shouldn't have said that to her. She was determined, though, and kept on taking me.

I went to Ontario High. I had my power wheelchair and getting around was easier. There was a long dirt road we had to go along to get to the house, and it was so bumpy. I never wanted to sit in the back of the school bus because if I did, I would bounce high in the air even with my seat belt on. I had to get up at 5:30–5:45 am every morning to get ready for the bus. It came at 6:00 am.

It was tougher emotionally; physically it wasn't as difficult as junior high because high school was a place to grow up, make friends, form relationships, play sports, go to dances, get a driver's license, hang out with friends outside of school, and go to prom.

I knew I had to be in the Special Ed Class, not for academic help, but more for the physical help. My teacher was Marti Schneider. She was the coolest teacher I had. I had other Special Ed teachers as well. My Special Ed teachers were the nicest teachers at Ontario High. They were my "school moms." An example of their kindness still sticks out in my mind: there was one student who was poor. They all chipped in and bought his family a Thanksgiving dinner. And on

Christmas, they had a Christmas party at school, and they gave him all the leftovers. I wasn't able to attend because I had regular Ed classes at that time. One day during winter he came to school with a thin jacket on, and it was freezing outside. One of my Special Ed teachers (Ms. Marge) gave him her Ontario High School letterman jacket. These are just some of the things they did to make his life more bearable—all spontaneous and generous.

One of the teachers encouraged me to work hard and finish my regular homework before I started goofing around. The problem was that most of the time I finished my work too fast and had nothing else to do. *My boring life.* Then when I got home, I had nothing else to work on. I couldn't help on the farm. There was just the big house to roll around in.

There were benefits to being in Special Ed sometimes. On Fridays, full-time students had a free day to do as they pleased. Students also received a free brunch meal every day. The assistants would always go and get regular milk, chocolate milk, bagels, muffins, apple and orange juice, and a lot of cream cheese. There were always leftovers, so they could make cheesecake and ice cream. Since I had mostly regular Ed classes, I had to work on Fridays and missed all the yummy treats.

Academically, I've always set high standards for myself. I took all outside classes (normal classes), and did my best to get straight A's. I was able to show the disabled students, the regular students, and especially the teachers that I wasn't going to let MD win. Our school motto was, *"Aim high, then aim higher."*

I have to admit there were times when it got too difficult to handle and I felt like giving up, and letting Muscular Dystrophy win completely. I couldn't experience all the joys of being a teenager. I just tried to ignore all the things I couldn't do. I focused on my academics. It was there that I found solace.

It's easier for everyone around me if I put on a smile. I know this because there was an incident where I went to school depressed and it had an interesting conclusion. My Special Ed teachers and their students were used to seeing me with a smile on my face. I was always making them laugh. That day I didn't say anything. Mrs. Schneider had a talk with me to see what was going on. She said that all her students were affected by my action of being depressed. I wouldn't have thought that I could have an impact on others. The students were also somewhat depressed because I didn't laugh or make them laugh. I didn't know that. Someone had to set an example for the others, and Mrs. Schneider believed that I could do that. So each day I always joked around, making them laugh, so the atmosphere in the class was always bright. I showed them that it's okay to have MD, cerebral palsy or other disabilities. Life isn't over just because you are disabled.

When I was fifteen, my scoliosis (curvature in the normally straight vertical line of the spine) got worse. I had to get a spinal fusion (using rods and wires, of all my vertebrae from my lower neck to my pelvis), which made everything worse for me. Before the surgery, I was able to do most things on my own without my mom's help. I was stronger before the surgery. I could get on and off my power wheelchair, the bath chair, toilet, and the bed. I was able to sleep on my back instead of on my side, and my hip was much straighter. After surgery, everything became more difficult for me because I wasn't able to keep doing those things on my own. As time passed, I had gotten weaker. I missed being able to do those things on my own. I knew what would happen if I didn't get the surgery. My spine would eventually curve and put pressure on my organs and diaphragm, making it harder to breathe. For the long term benefits, I decided to go ahead with it. It was my decision to get the surgery, not my parents'.

There was one student in high school that didn't get the back surgery because of religious reasons, so his back was curved so much that it was beyond repair. Consequently, he had to have a special back support modified on his chair to make him comfortable.

I really don't have anyone that I'd call a best friend in high school, but I did once, Jake Demy. We hung out at school whenever I had free time. He was in the special program too. He moved to Colorado after his sophomore year. I don't think he would remember me if he is still alive because he had a brain deterioration disease. He looked fine to me when he was attending Ontario High. Hanging around and knowing someone with a disease is scary at times because you don't know how much they'll deteriorate. It gave me a different perspective on my own disease. I'm always on the inside looking out. This time I was on the outside looking in. Jake gave me the strength to go on and I realized how fortunate I was compared to him.

I won a special scholar award; I believe that Mrs. Marti Schneider (Special Ed teacher) had something to do with it. I attended 1-2 special ed. classes like P.E. and study hall; I was part of the school's (Ontario High) Renaissance Program. It was based on academics. The school had a rally for our award ceremonies; Mrs. Schneider had secretly invited my mom. I didn't even know I was getting an award. To be honest, I didn't want to attend the ceremony; but Mrs. Schneider insisted that I attend. The school presented my award toward the end of the ceremony. I was the first disabled student to get that award, and the first to get that award in the Special Ed program, so I was pretty much representing the Special Ed program. You would think that I'd be excited, but I wasn't. It just felt the same as any other award I got for academics. I was thinking, *They only gave me this award because I'm in a wheelchair.* After I received my award, both Mrs. Schneider and my mom cried.

We had to do a senior research paper to graduate. My senior term paper was about Muscular Dystrophy. My thesis was about how "normal" people assume that people in wheelchairs have had a car accident and have cognitive impairments. When I was doing the research, my brother, Jason, and Nick Calagna (a friend) said, "You're just going to make yourself depressed." I felt it was best that I understood what I had, so I could better prepare myself for what the future might hold for me. I didn't have that much on BMD because it's similar to DMD, but slower. The report was only thirteen pages long. My final was an oral report of the paper. Most of the students' reports were only five minutes long and boring. My report lasted thirty-five minutes, but the students didn't lose interest in what I had to say. No one had their head down or wiggled in their seats. They were surprised to learn what I had because they didn't know that I had MD. I got an A+ on my final. The students were scared to ask me questions though.

My Senior English teacher, Kelly Jean Higdon Olivas, nominated me Student of the Month for the English department. I didn't know that I was her favorite student until some of the students told me. She was a cool teacher because she didn't care what I was doing in her class, as long as I finished my work. I wanted to prove to all the teachers, especially Mrs. Schneider, that I could earn the grades and awards myself. I just wanted to prove to them that I was a normal student. I endangered my health to do it. Despite all the hard work, I still felt that I was never seen as a normal student. My brother, Jason, said that I got an "A" in her class because she felt sorry for me. I don't feel that. I felt that I earned it.

During our pre-prom activities, when the A.S.B. announced the candidates for King's Court on the loud speaker in front of the whole school, I heard my name, yet I wasn't excited. I wondered why I was nominated. All I knew was that the court was based on grades, popularity, and attitude at school. There are more reasons, but I don't know the rest. When everyone congratulated me, I said to myself, "*So what?*" I thanked him or her though. The other candidates were excited, but I already knew that I wouldn't win, and I didn't want to. It wasn't important to me.

I went to prom, not because I wanted to; it was because I was on Prom Court, and it would go on my transcript. Even though I went with a date, I was still lonely and hurting because I couldn't do what everyone else could. I didn't really care if I won or not. It was really bad for me emotionally, but I hid it from my date. I didn't want to ruin it for her because she took the time to go with me. I wanted to really have a relationship with someone. I shouldn't have gone, but I knew that I was representing the Special Ed program.

I asked one of my friends from junior high to go with me to my Senior Prom, Rin Harts; she still lived down in Lakeside. I wore a white suit, and it was too big for me. Rin wore a sparkling black dress. My date and I sat by ourselves and needless to say I found out a lot of things about my friends that evening. In a way I was testing their friendship to see if they would sit at the same table as me, but they didn't. I didn't try to sit with them because I felt that I wasn't important enough to them, so why bother? I tried not to pay attention to everyone dancing and having a good time; if I had, it would have really gotten depressing for me. I didn't want to make Rin depressed either. It was the first time I opened my heart to someone, just a little.

I enjoyed spending time talking to Rin. The nicest part about her was that she took the time to drive all the way up to go to the prom with me. We were served chicken for dinner. She cut my chicken into little bite size pieces; she took off the skin too. Then we had a big slice of chocolate cake; too much chocolate. I didn't win King's Court, and Prom night was the toughest experience I had to endure up until then. When we went back home, she fell asleep in the car, so I just watched her as she slept. I wanted to put my sports jacket on her because it was cold in there. While watching her I began thinking to myself that I would never get to experience being in a relationship. That made me melancholy. The next day I wrote her a long thank you letter.

Rin said she had a better time at my prom than at her prom because her boyfriend was a jerk. All he wanted to do was spend that time with his friends and not her. I believe he was a year older than she. We had pictures taken and I actually ran out of them because everyone wanted one. I had split half of the pictures with Rin because I knew she'd pass the rest out to my friends back in Lakeside.

Because of the surgery, I wasn't going to graduate on time. Even though I had extra credits, I was missing a semester of P.E., so the only way I was going to graduate with my class was if my P.E. teacher would agree to give me credit for some of the time I was absent. *What do I need P.E. for anyway?*

Realistically, I could have stayed in high school until I was twenty-two. Most of the special education students stayed for that long, but a few wanted to finish high school in four years. I joked with Mrs. Schneider that I was planning to stay another four years with her. She didn't believe me, although; she did what she could to get me out of high school in four years. Mrs. Olivas said, "There won't be anything for you to learn if you stay." She was right. In spite of the obstacles, I graduated with the highest honors, yet I wasn't excited. To tell you the truth, it was just another day that went by. I was one of the few to graduate with highest honors in the Special Ed class, but it was cold sitting out there until the ceremony was over. I wondered what new beginnings lay in store for me.

I wanted Mrs. Schneider to be there at my graduation, but she had to take her mom to the hospital because she was suffering from cancer. This was the first year she wasn't able to attend. She wanted to be there, too.

I did think it strange that we didn't get our diplomas at the ceremony; it was right after the senior brunch. In addition, I didn't get a graduation gift like everyone else. My family did take me to eat to celebrate, but that was it. We had to pick up our diplomas the next day.

When I went to school the next day, Mrs. Schneider told me why she didn't attend. Then the other Special Ed teachers handed me a newspaper article they wanted me to read. I was disgusted with the article, just as they were. One of the students had done an interview with the local paper and said horrible things about the school, students, teachers, and especially the Special Ed department. She said the students were mean, the teachers were unfair, and that the school wasn't going to let people like her graduate like everyone else. Basically it was all about herself and her family. If they had interviewed me, I would have said the opposite of what she said. The teachers said, "How could she have said something like that?" I was the perfect example to prove her wrong. Those things never happened to me at school. I was treated like any other student. I didn't need special treatment, except some physical help.

I felt that the reason she said those things was because she was used to having everything her way. She was spoiled, like many special education students are. Some Special Ed students had the cognitive capacity to attend regular classes, but they didn't want to; they were just lazy. When something got too hard for them, they just quit. Plus, they always thought they could get away with bad behavior. If they couldn't pass the required tests, they would get another chance, but their tests were easier to begin with.

The local paper said the student was a heroine because she stood up for herself. I simply thought she was selfish. Because she was in a wheelchair, I think she and her family felt she wasn't treated as equally as the regular education students. *Hello? I am in a wheelchair and I felt like I was treated equally and with respect.*

## College

After high school, I attended Chaffey Community College in Alta Loma, California. I wanted to attend Cal Poly Pomona, but it was too far of a drive. College wasn't exciting to me and I lost interest in school. It's not like the classes were hard or anything. It was just hard physically and emotionally. I ignored the stares, but it was still too difficult to be around "normal" students all the time. Most of the time, I didn't say anything to others because I felt I had nothing interesting to talk about. I believe that they didn't say anything to me about everyday life because they knew I never got to do those things, and they didn't want to make it even more difficult than it was on me.

College is the place to choose your career, meet true friends, enjoy life, and get knowledge. Physically it was too difficult; all the classes I wanted were scheduled at night, so I couldn't take them. I got tired so fast, schooling took a lot out of me, and I still pushed the limits of my health. It took my mom away from her busy schedule as well. With that in mind, she didn't get anything done when I went to school (she drove me to and from campus; an hour roundtrip).

MD just takes so much energy out of me. My bottom was always sore from sitting all day. Because of the person I am, I didn't want to have my mom overdo everything, which she has a tendency to do. She's my mom and the only one in my family who can take the time to help me. My brothers and sister have their own busy schedules. They have to start their own lives before it's too late. It's the long term that I'm concerned about, so I don't ask for much out of them. They can fulfill their dreams first, and then they should take care of my mom, so she doesn't have to work as hard.

Another reason I didn't continue going to college was that even if I completed college, I had no idea what I'd be able to do with that knowledge. It was a waste of time going if I wasn't going to get to use it. I had huge ambitions in life. I wanted to go to a university instead of a community college and live on campus and enjoy being on my own (enjoying campus life) without my parents supporting me. After graduation, I would have moved out and lived on my own with my high paying job. I would have given my parents enough of my paycheck, so they wouldn't have to worry about money in their retirement. I really wanted them to use the money to have fun because my parents didn't have the chance to go out and have fun while they both worked and raised two disabled boys.

I was going to take at least twenty units a semester in college. I wanted to finish college early and go to graduate school and take the exam to become a CPA. It didn't turn out that way. It's more like I gave up my schooling to make my mom's life easier. I didn't want her to keep driving me. The bus system stinks. All the places I needed to go, I had to depend on everyone else to take me. Most of this fell on my mom. My dreams died a long time ago. In school, the teachers always told us that we could obtain all our dreams if we put our minds to it. That doesn't help me. We moved to Norco, California afterward.

# 4. Observations

This chapter contains my take on life and the devastation MD has had on my body and mind. I was home and bored all the time. I had time to think about stuff.

**Life**

Realistically I should have little hope left in life, but life without hope is meaningless. You're nothing more than an empty shell without emotions whatsoever. Sometimes I think, *Why bother trying to enjoy life if I can't do anything?* In little ways, I guess that means I have given up. It's just that it is terrifying not knowing your future. Will I live at home forever? How fast will my physical condition deteriorate? Until MD takes over completely, I must accept my declining abilities. Why did I have to realize all this so soon?

As for my desires in life, I really don't have that many. I still desire to help my mom out as much as I can; I read her mail; I make all the household appointments and I maintain the IHSS (The IHSS Program will help pay for services provided to you so that you can remain safely in your own home) time sheets. I tell myself that I shouldn't worry about what will happen to me in the future. It's what I can do for her now that is important. One day I won't be able to do anything for her.

Life with MD is very hard because I can't do that much for myself physically. I also know that I will always have to depend on others. Most of the time, I feel that I'm trapped inside my body, a body that doesn't work as it should. I always have to depend on someone to do things for me: like the bathroom, shower, bed, and even getting something to eat. MD doesn't just affect me, it affects everyone around me. My mom takes it the hardest because she feels that it was her fault, and she can't do anything about how my life has turned out so far. That's why she gets frustrated and upset. I don't take her frustration personally because I know that it is not her fault.

It's also hard for me to show my feelings to my mom, because I know how hard it is for her. My mom gets upset even hearing or talking about MD. I try to make it as easy as I can for her. I don't ask her to take me anywhere like the movies, eating out, or going to the mall, etc. If I have to go somewhere important, I can depend on her though.

I spend a lot of time observing people. Most don't realize what they have, and I'll often hear them complaining about their lives, and yet they have normal bodies and brain capacity. They don't know what it's like to have an impaired body. They just choose not to enjoy what they have. They should just change their attitudes toward life and try to enjoy it. If people want a better life, they should just go out and make it happen instead of complaining. They should be grateful for what they have. That's my take on things at least.

## Day to Day Life

I'm always bored, but not out of my mind and not to the point of complaining about it. I easily lose interest in things I do. When I play video games with Jason, I lose interest. It's the same with reading a book, sometimes watching a movie, and sometimes when I go out. I try to keep the monotony out of my mind, so I always find something to do, even if it's a small activity. Most of the times, I just roll around the house. Jason tells me that I'm dull.

I want to travel and see the world, but I'm stuck at home. I only get to see different places of the world on TV, magazines, and the Internet. That's not the same as actually being there. I would be able to smell the air, see the hustle and bustle of the world. I'd be able to eat different types of foods that I've never heard of or have seen before, and meet new people and experience their cultures. The places I really want to go see are Japan, China, Sweden or Ireland. I want to go to Japan because of all the anime I watch, the setting is in Japan, and I really want to see the cherry blossom petals falling on the ground on a windy day. In China, I want to experience my culture at the heart of it. Sweden or Ireland, to see the grasslands they both have. Maybe in Ireland, I could catch a leprechaun and get lucky! I wouldn't want their gold! Traveling and meeting different people are memories for a lifetime.

I don't like staying home all the time; once in a while I would like to go out and do something, but not by myself of course. Although, in some ways I don't mind being here because every time I go out people stare at me.

When people ask me why I'm in wheelchair, they would always say, "Were you in a car accident?" I tell them I have MD, and most of them don't know what it is. It was natural for me to explain the aspects of the disease to people and not get nervous because I've done it so many times before. They all seemed to be interested in what I had to say, and they were too scared to ask me questions.

When people see my power wheelchair, they always tell me that they want one as well and I always think, *Yeah right*. That's easy for them to say because when they get tired of the wheelchair, they can just get up and walk. When people have to be in a wheelchair for awhile (like with a broken leg), I see them upset or frustrated. Most of the time, I want to tell them to just get over it. It's not like they're in the wheelchair permanently. In a few months they'll get better and end up getting out of the wheelchair. As for me, in a few months, I'll still be in a wheelchair.

**Changes**

Now eating a meal is harder for me because it's difficult to lift my arms up. I'm always the last one to finish. Most of the time, I'm a messy eater. I can only use one hand to eat. My other arm helps support my eating arm. When I lean forward to eat, I can only hold that position for a short period of time, so I take a bite of food and immediately push myself back up. I do that for every bite. When I want to eat something, and it's in a bag, I can't open it. I always say, "Can't open it, can't eat it." I have to wait for someone to open it. My mom always asks me, "You want to eat?" and I say, "No." After the fourth time she asks me, I'll eat it.

I depend on someone to help me. I hate bothering others, but I know that I need assistance. It's really frustrating when I have to go to the bathroom in the middle of the night, and I can't get out of bed on my own. I have no choice but to wake up my mom. I don't drink that much at night because of that reason. She gets angry at me and says hurtful words. I don't blame her because I know that I just woke her up. I feel that I'm just a burden to her, though. I get so upset sometimes that I just cry myself to sleep. It's hard for me to sleep and I've never slept through a night without having to wake up to adjust or reposition myself. It hurts most of the time because I end up lying in the same position throughout the night. It's frustrating because my body doesn't respond. If there's an itch I can't do anything about that either, but it does keep me up for a while. Then I just ignore it and go to sleep. My mom usually gets me up before she leaves for work.

I often get frustrated at MD, and I have negative thoughts about having it. I end up not wanting to do anything the next day. Some days, I don't want to get out of bed. I just want to lie there and sleep in late, but I always end up dragging myself out of bed. I don't want to, but I must. That just shows that I still want to do something, even if the day does seem to be the same as yesterday.

I get frustrated sometimes when people go out without having to wait on others. I can't just go out whenever I want. I can't just get ready without any help from my mom or someone. I can't even drive; I can't get a call from someone to go hang out and just go without any hesitations. When I do go out with others, they end up having to wait on me and take care of me. I feel that I'm a burden on their fun. I also feel that they don't get to do what they want because it's a hassle to get me in and out the car. That's why no one asks me to go anywhere; that's what I believe. There are all these obstacles in my way, and I can't expect others to put up with that.

It's also hard at times because I can't tell my mom or Jason my feelings because I know how they will react. I just keep it from them. I don't want to see my mom cry. It'll make Jason angry, and he'll make it difficult for my mom because she can't fix either of us. When my friends ask me to talk to Jason about MD, I tell them that I shouldn't because it'll make it worse for him. I don't usually show my frustrations and pains around people. There have been times where I have shown them. Maybe that's when I'm not as strong as I think I am. It gets hard sometimes being an island.

In order to keep myself going I've developed certain interests. I love to watch anime. I started watching anime when I was eleven years old. It is a type of Japanese animation. I'm so enthralled by it that I believe everyone should watch them because they all carry a message. Most of them are real-life situations. Since my contact with the world is limited, I have to learn in other ways and I have learned a lot from watching it. The shows teach me how to be a better person, no matter what the situation may be. My favorite anime of all time is "Macross II," and I've watched it too many times. (*The Superdimensional Fortress Macross II*)

There was an anime with two girls talking about which personality is their true self because they have two different personalities when they use their powers. I'm stuck with the same situation. Which side of me is my true self: the normal or the MD side? To be honest, I believe that my true self is my MD side. When I'm thinking with MD, it brings out the best in me and helps me become a better person and make better judgments in life. There is a difference between the two sides: the normal side of my thinking tends to be on the negative side (the "whys" and the "ifs"), and the MD side of my thinking is the positive side of it all with acceptance of my life.

Some of my family members say I have anger inside. I believe so too. I rarely show that side of me to others. I'm just angry at stuff that I can't change. I don't take it out on others; I just say what they need to hear, but most don't want to hear it. It's necessary to say it to them. It looks like I am angry, but they don't take me seriously. I'm always in a good mood because I'm not thinking about anything. I try so hard not to let my anger come out in front of my mom, but one time, I told her that I need to be repositioned on the seat to use the restroom, and she said, "Why you always need to be repositioned all the time?" I got angry a bit, and I said, "You don't know what it's like because you don't have any difficulty using the restroom." I know that I shouldn't say that. I learned not to hold on to my anger and just let it go. Being angry won't change anything.

MD makes me exert all my energy really fast. It takes energy just to do the littlest things in my daily life. To most people, they wouldn't think it takes so much energy to do the small things. Throughout the day, I look half asleep, but I get at least nine to ten hours of sleep each day. You may think I need to exercise to raise my stamina, but I do exercise each day by doing things on my own. Even eating is an exercise to me, and I get so tired. Going out to eat at a restaurant is a lot more difficult for me, not chewing or swallowing; it's getting the food up to my mouth. I do try to enjoy my meal. Most of the times I just want to finish my meal quickly, so I don't have to exert all my energy all at once.

Most people are embarrassed when they go out with me, even some of my family members. I can tell by their looks, and I do ask them. Their answer is "Yes." I don't get mad about it, which means I don't care what others think about me. I'm just acting myself when I go out. They probably don't have problems with who I am, but rather what others may think about how I act when I'm out in public.

## Medical Equipment

Medical equipment is difficult to get these days. Most families with some type of a physical disability don't have medical insurance, so most of us rely on the government for medical insurance, Medi-Cal. I have had that for a long time and I have a difficult time getting the equipment that I need. It's all that paperwork and waiting for approval. It takes forever for them to decide if the equipment is necessary for my condition. Who are they to make that kind of assessment for me? They're not the physical therapists or the doctors. I know there are people out there that misuse their medical insurances and their equipment, but most are honest about what they need.

It would be cheaper if the government would approve our equipment faster. Without the equipment we need, our conditions get worse and worse, causing us to go to the emergency room or the hospital. The hospital bills are expensive these days. It ends up costing Medi-Cal more when the equipment could have prevented the need to go to the hospital in the first place. For example, getting a hospital bed with a special type of mattress that would prevent open bed

38

sores. It only cost a few thousand dollars for that. On the other hand, having the open bed sore would cost tens and even hundreds of thousands of dollars for hospital expenses. It's just common sense. It's all about the money these days. If you don't have money, you could end up dying.

## The Meaning of Life

What's my purpose in life, anyway? With MD, I can't always tell what that is. I do believe I'm here for a reason. My sense of purpose in life is: to be an example for Jason's reaction to his own MD; to show my mom that it isn't her fault that I have this disease by not giving up on life; to be an inspiration for others; and to help change one person's way of looking at life through MD. If I can at least change one person's way of thinking, then I'm satisfied with my sense of purpose in life.

## Suicide

Even with having MD, I never have thought of committing suicide.

"Suicide is a part of reality, caused by anger, at or from another person, the world, the universe, love, a failure or God. Others are caused by great sadness and emotional pain. People see suicide as the only way to stop their pain or sadness. There are other kinds of suicides out there too. One kind of suicide is to stop living. Not everyone asks for help when they need it because they may not know how to. Family and friends are the ones who need to be alert and offer their help to their loved ones who are thinking about suicide. I believe that people should look at different individual's behaviors instead of just making light of the problems. Then we have to help pull them out of the doldrums. Even a little bit of reaching out helps." ("Death Be Not Whatever")

Even so, on the subject of suicide it's hard for me to comprehend why other people take the easy way out from their problems, especially if they are normal (with a healthy body and normal brain capacity) unless they're in excruciating pain that won't go away ever. They don't seem to realize that what they're going to do will cause extreme pain to their family and friends. Some of the living may not be able to get through the loss of a love one, and they might do the same thing. That's just sad. Every problem can be solved no matter how difficult it may seem; they just have to try all possible solutions to overcome their problem that they are going through.

I emphatically believe that we human beings are strong when a disaster happens to us, that we human beings will help each other to become stronger. For example, in WWII when the U.S. dropped two atomic bombs on Japan to end the war, it didn't cause Japan to crumble. Japan didn't let that stop them from being one of the top technological countries in the world. The way I look at it, the best way to live life is to live life with struggles and pains as well as happiness. Without those experiences, people tend to take their lives for granted. "To have a good life, people have to act on their emotions," ("Zero wan bakuha shirei") but they cannot let their emotions take control of them. I strongly believe that, because hiding emotions can only lead to ruin and despair later on, eventually leading to suicide.

## Death

My attitude about death is that I'm not scared of dying. I think about death like this. If there is a life after death, then there is no death. If death does not exist, we do not live. That could be true. Then there is no reason to fear death. Death is just another journey that we have to take eventually. Death is something I've embraced. Death is a part of life. Fearing death will only stop you from living. Death will meet up with you sooner or later. Some people who live, deserve to die; some people who die deserve to live. Life and death aren't fair.

All living things die eventually. We don't know when our time comes or how it will happen, either. All we can do is live our lives to the best of our abilities. I embrace this even if there isn't that much I can do with my limitations. Do what you can now. I know that my life will end due to respiratory or cardiac failure. I always tell myself that when my life is over there will be one less person that my mom has to take care of or worry about.

I told my mom that she should just cremate me. It's cheaper. I want my ashes to be carried away with the wind, so I can be everywhere. Free at last.

At my funeral, I wouldn't want anyone to cry for me. I want people to have peaceful expressions, not because I'm gone, but because I want people to remember how I affected and inspired their lives in one way or another. Who knows, maybe I'll be watching. I won't be completely separated from this world because people who have had the chance to get to know me will always carry a part of me in their hearts. I hope to have made a difference to at least one person. If I have made a difference to one person's life and one's heart, I can leave with a smile.

## Religious Background, Children and Friends

Although my family is Buddhist, they aren't very religious. So I never thought about life on a spiritual level. I'm not a spiritual person. To me, all religion is the same because in the end we will have to go somewhere.

I believe someone put me on this earth to watch all the experiences of other people. My perspective on my life is that I'm here for everyone else, not for myself. I'm living with MD to teach everyone around me. People think that it's great and all, but who in their right mind would want that responsibility? I know I sure don't . . . but I live with it here and now. I'm not trying to be strong about it or wanting to inspire people with my life, I'm just living and enjoying what time I have left, and taking every opportunity that opens up for me. I live with MD and it's okay . . . adapting to life . . . with laughter.

## Having Children

Have I ever thought about having children? Yes, I have thought about having children in the future. My children won't get MD, either boy or girl. I'm the victim, not the carrier. I would love to have a daughter named Rin, but since my daughter would become a carrier of MD, just having her would give me a tremendous sense of guilt. In turn, she would have the heavy burden of deciding whether to have children or not, and it would not be my choice to make. It would be my daughter's decision.

How can I have children if I can't be a father to them? For instance doing the things a father usually does, protecting the family from danger, financial support, etc. How can I have a family of my own if I can't physically interact with them? I can't do that to them. It is an immature wish and I know that, but if I did have children I would teach them to be their own person with their own views and understanding of the world. I'd get them to interact with all types of people: every race, gays, the elderly, as well as mentally and physically challenged individuals. By doing that, they'd be able to understand that we are all equal. I would want them to grow up without worrying about what others say about them and to be responsible for what they do. Most of all, I would want them to have a sense of humor. I would also pass on my dreams, my views, and heart to them.

# 5. Relationships

## Friendships

If you don't interact with your friends or call them then you'll probably lose their friendship. I truly believe that. That's pretty much why I lost most of my friends. They stopped calling me back. I'm not upset or angry with them. I'm not blaming anyone either. It's just that the lack of communication caused me to give up on their friendship. Furthermore, I never really hang out with anyone. I believe it's because people don't get to see the kind of person I really am. MD seems to shroud me in mystery.

As I got older, I notice that I seem to be the one to initiate a conversation. Even when acquaintances are online, I always have to say "Hi" first. It comes with the disease. Sometimes I am invisible. It's the same for my brother. Jason asked me, "Why do I always have to say 'Hi' first?" I told him that it's always been like that for me. It seems like my friends forgot about me. I stopped checking my emails every day. I don't put the same amount of effort into friendship as I used to.

I guess I've learned to let friendships go and not worry about having or not having everything that I would like. Making a big deal of it will only end with pain and sadness, so I don't think about how it should be. I concentrate on keeping the friends that do want my friendship; it's not just what they say, it's their actions that show me that they care. To me, the most rewarding experience about having friends is having a conversation with them on the phone, not chit-chatting. Letting go is difficult, but that's the only way to move on and really cherish the good friends that I do have.

## Friendships of the Heart

I met Joan and Ashly late February of 2000, through my brother, Jason. Joan and Ashly were my brother's physical and occupational therapists. Joan was the physical therapist and Ashly was the occupational therapist; two sisters working at the same place at the time. They were always together, best friends.

## Joan Allin

I didn't know much about her really. She didn't tell me much about herself. It was her actions that showed me who she really was, though I rarely got to see her.

She was the kind of person that said whatever was on her mind and was not afraid to say it. When she got mad at me, she told me and didn't hide it. Yet she was a kind and caring person as well. She often helped me with medical equipment and she always gave me the option on which equipment I could use. I know she had other patients to take care of, which means she had work to do but she always found time to help me out.

## Ashly Allin

She was caring, compassionate, hard-working, kind, easy-going, fun to hang out with, had a sense of humor, but she was not very good at hiding her emotions. Ashly became like one of my best friends because she started coming over for lunch once a week after Jason quit being her patient. She bought lunch for Jason and me. She worked a few minutes away from us and we'd spend time catching up on each other's lives.

We also talked about life situations with MD and how difficult it was for my brother and me. Ashly had a hard time responding to my questions. I'd always tell her, "I know you don't have the answers, and it's okay." I'd give her answers even though they were tough to hear.

## Venturing Out

Once Joan, Ashly, Jason, and I went to the mall and had dinner. We probably were there at the restaurant for more than two hours. I ordered for everyone because I wanted to do that at least once in this lifetime. Joan was impressed. She commented, "And we thought we had you figured out." Jason didn't talk much. He left most of his vegetables untouched, and Ashly was eating them. The vegetables were on the other side of the plate. It was funny. Then I told him to turn his plate around. What came later was special. When I was ordering, I had also ordered a slice of cheesecake. The waiter came out with a big plate with four forks, and we shared it piece by piece. Joan enjoyed it the most. I wanted to pay the bill, but they didn't let me.

One of the most memorable events in my life was when my brother and I were invited to attend Ashly's wedding in March of 2003. The ceremony was held at a neighborhood church along the coast, in Palos Verdes, California, where her parents had married as well. It was exquisite; it had a beautiful view of the ocean. At her reception, the entertainment consisted of Hawaiian music and hula dancing. It was fun, and the dancing was very good. What I remember the most about that evening was the part where Ashly performed a hula dance for her husband. Everyone was focused on Ashly, but I was focused on her sister as well. Joan was in tears. It must have been a touching moment for her. That showed me how caring she was. Joan was the happiest person there because of her happiness for Ashly. She wanted us to be a part of her life.

As time went by, I just let our friendship take its own course. Eventually we had a great friendship with each other. Joan was the first friend that yelled at me when I got on her nerves. I'm grateful that she didn't keep that from me because when people get mad at me, they don't say anything because they believe that because I'm in a wheelchair it might make it worse for me. That's not good because then I won't know what I've done wrong, and I would keep on doing the same thing. If they don't tell me, then they're not treating me as a normal friend.

When Joan yelled at me about the shower I'd been complaining about, I realized that I had to do something about it. I really wanted my mom to have a walk-in shower, and she didn't want to get it because she didn't have money for it. I raised the money all by myself in one day. I explained the situation in an email to my Uncle Bobby, my brother Steven and my friend Tai Sam. I asked them specifically because I knew each would be sympathetic to the cause and I could count on them. What I didn't realize was that each of them would give so much. They did this because they loved my mom. My brother realized that my mom really needed that shower, because he knew what my mom had to do for my brother and me. Tai was a good family friend. At first, my mom didn't believe I raised the money for the shower, so I showed her. She was ecstatic and my parents had no objections to whichever shower proposal I chose.

Joan and Ashly were two wonderful people, and two wonderful friends. I never had any friends like them before. They treated me as a normal friend. They showed me that they wanted to hang out with me, and it wasn't just because I asked. I met two more friends, and one of them became my best friend.

I met Aria Palachi at one of my MDA clinic appointments at Loma Linda University Health Care. She was Italian and around my age. She was a student physical therapist. It happened to be at the time that I had started sharing my story. She was quiet, but she listened carefully to the patients. I was a bit shy because she was pretty. I know my brother, Jason, checked her out. I didn't do that; instead I focused on asking Dr. Reid all the questions that I needed answers for. Afterwards, I offered to share my story with him. Aria suddenly piped in and asked me if I would share it with her as well. I nodded and she gave me her email.

Aria and I became friends after that. It took emailing back and forth for us to really get to know each other. Our computers became important because she graduated from Loma Linda

University a month after I met her and moved back home to Sonoma County, California. That's quite a distance from Norco, California. Thank goodness for technology. We used to email each other often, at least once a week. It was refreshing.

## David Erickson

I met David Erickson at the Muscular Dystrophy Association Clinic in 2000. He is the Occupational Therapist Consultant for the clinic. When I offered my work-in-progress autobiography, he gladly took it, and our friendship went from there. For a few years, we only saw each other a few times a year but would email each other back and forth. I was told by others that my thoughts were deep, but his thoughts were deeper than mine. He gave very insightful answers to the questions I asked him. I may not understand them completely. I took them all to heart but I was never able to physically put them in motion. I've learned from him instead of learning through my hardships or on my own.

## A True Friend

When does a true friend come into one's life? A true friend can come or start from anywhere; from chance, from destiny, from fate, from God, from hope, from luck, from a prayer, from a tragedy, from a wish or just out of the blue.

"A true friend is the greatest of all blessings, and that which we take the least care of all to acquire." (Francois de La Rochefoucauld)

Anyone can be a true friend to another, and yet they're so hard to come by. Many may never have someone to call a true

When we have a true friend in our lives, we end up doing more for each other than we necessarily have to think about doing. We end up experiencing so much that can change us, but having a true friend around can prevent us from changing into someone other than who we really are. Getting through so many experiences, good or bad, with one another will definitely deepen and strengthen the bond, becoming more like close siblings.

"Do you know what friendship is? It is to be brother and sister; two souls which touch without mingling, two fingers on one hand." (Victor Hugo)

People end up setting up expectations on themselves to be a better person for each other. Some set expectations and some set higher expectations on themselves without knowing it. A true friend isn't perfect. No one is. With expectations, people tend to let each other down. Expectations cause disappointments big or small. A true friend may get angry, disappointed, hurt, or upset, but when they forgive or show forgiveness, their bond strengthens between each other.

Appreciation of a true friend may be tiny or big, but mostly, appreciation from the other isn't necessarily said or shown. It may just be too difficult to describe an appreciation of a friend. There are even those who feel that words cannot clearly show or tell their appreciation. That just means that a true friend had an overwhelming impact in one's heart and life. There's always the phrase, "Thank you." Just those two little words can mean a great deal. Always let a true friend know how much he or she is appreciated every now and then. It doesn't take long to do. All it takes is a few minutes. It doesn't have to be big and fancy. A simple gesture or a thank you works just as much.

A true friend isn't measured by how much one can have such as money or earthly status or physical talents or physical traits. It's measured in how much, big or small, one will do for the other—sacrifices made, trust for each other, empathy, sympathy and love.

"True friends are the connection of spirit that makes lifelong friends, not bodies. It matters not what we look like, or what we can do. It matters only that friends form that common bond that cannot be broken by material life here." (David Erickson, friend)

"Remember, the greatest gift is not found in a store nor under a tree, but in the hearts of true friends." (Cindy Lew)

## Relationships

I am lonely all the time even though I'm around my family all the time. That's still not the same as spending time with someone special. I want to truly share my heart with someone. My heart has all these wonderful words to say, but I won't get to say them.

Do you believe that there is someone out there for everyone, like a soul mate? Or that not everyone has a soul mate? Liking someone and being in love with someone are two totally different things. I can't fully share my heart with anyone because no one will feel the same way about me. I won't give up on that idea as long as I have the will to want a relationship. "To live a full life is to act on your emotions" ("Saigo no Shôrisha"). I won't know if I don't act on my emotions. It's better to find out the answer than regretting it when your life is over.

For me, having a relationship is like wanting to touch the brightest star out there. Just reaching for that shiny star is impossible for me. I feel that my shiny star is moving away from my grasp. I'm almost there, but no matter what I do, that shiny star will always be just a little bit beyond my reach. But I have to keep on trying.

Maybe not in this lifetime, but in the next life, I will find someone and be able to fully share my heart with someone. I really believe that the soul is forever because everyone on earth has a different personality.

This is hard for me to deal with because it's not like I could keep my mind off of this subject. Love is everywhere: in the movies, going out, books, magazines, at home, anime, and even songs. Watching people having the experiences of being in a relationship gets to me most of the time. There are things I want to experience in a relationship. I want to call or see someone just for no reason at all, hold someone's hand, look in her eyes, watch her sleep, run my fingers through her hair, watching the stars together, stuff like that. Two things I really want from a relationship are having a dance with her and experiencing my first kiss, but most important is just being with her.

My ideal date would be she and I having a candlelight dinner outside on a clear night's sky with the moon shining brightly with the stars. Then after the dinner, I'll ask her to close her eyes, and then I'll get out of my chair and stand up in front of her. I'll ask her for a dance. With the moon shining brightly with the stars, we could see each other clearly, and we'll be dancing under the stars. I want to twirl her around which will make her dress spin. Then we could relax watching the stars together lying on the ground. Then I'll whisper in her ear and say, "I wish this could last forever." When the date is over, I'll give her a sweet gentle kiss.

Trying is the only way to experience life. I may have what it takes on the inside, but I don't have what it takes on the outside. I wasn't talking about looks or being in a wheelchair or not being able to walk. I mean that I can't do anything for myself physically.

I don't want someone wishing that she could give me the same things and experiences as a normal relationship has to offer. I don't want her to go out with me on a date and feel that she wishes that I could do normal activities like everyone else.

If someone did feel the same way about me, I wouldn't push her away. Even if we go beyond a friendship, I don't want her to have a life with MD. It's just not fair for her. I can't bear to see someone wishing for something for me. To have a relationship like that with me, someone will have to truly understand what she would have to get into. If that person still gives me that chance, then it will be of her own free will.

This is a burden I have to live with. It'll be a difficult burden to carry in life, but I'll be strong and face it. I'm just letting my life take its own course. I'm glad that I got to experience being in love. If it happens then great, but if it doesn't, then, "Oh well."

**Love**

I feel that I should talk about this subject, even if it hurts me to do so. I know how difficult, lonesome, and painful love can be.

Love can be the greatest feeling or the greatest pain in the universe. It depends on what side of love you end up with. Love is too painful. Many may say otherwise because love is going their way, but what about the people who can't catch love? Love is balance; there are winners and losers.

Love can bring out the best or the worst in someone. There are no guarantees what will happen to a person when rejected by love. Every one seeks love. Love is the greatest power in this world; it is the essence of life. You can't live without it; life will have no meaning when there is no love. If you are rejected, then either sadness or fear surrounds your being.

I've chased after love a few times, and I have always been turned down. I can honestly say this, "Love is a double-edge sword." I used to believe, "It's not what's on the outside that matters; but it's what's on the inside that matters." It's actually the other way around. Looks come first; everything else is noticed afterward. No one will give you a chance or notice you if that person isn't attractive to you. When it comes down to it, their actions show differently. People have to be attractive to someone in order to give a person a chance. Then that person will want to know everything about that person: their strengths and weaknesses, likes and dislikes, and character and heart. Then that person will love that person for who they are.

What makes love so hard to deal with is that I've been doing what most normal people do and thinking like a normal person. I would tend to fall in love with a normal girl. I wouldn't chase after a normal girl if I wasn't around normal people all the time. What I mean is that if I was always around other people like myself, I would be interested in them and not normal people.

Having a normal brain capacity makes it so hard. Well, then again if I didn't have a normal brain capacity, I wouldn't have to think about love. Wouldn't that be less painful to not know about love? But I know I'm fortunate to be able to tell what love takes and how wonderful love can be.

I'll still try chasing love because, "Time is too slow for those who wait, too swift for those who fear, but for those who love, time is eternity" (Henry Van Dyke). Being hesitant won't get me anywhere. I don't know for certain if that's what will happen if I don't go for it. Love can be difficult, but the future is still uncertain. I know I'll regret it if I don't take a step forward. Get the courage to just go for it; even if it'll be painful at the end, at least I'll know what the outcome is. Life without pain is no life at all.

Being in love with a normal girl is so complicated to deal with. I have to consider every possible reason before telling her my feelings. I'm chasing a girl for all the right reasons, but I end up seeing all the wrong reasons. Going forward, you have to ask yourself this question, "Are you willing to risk everything?" By everything, I mean the relationship which is formed, and losing that person in the process. If you're not willing to risk all that, then don't bother telling that person.

I'm willing to take those huge risks. I want to know if I'm capable of winning a girl's heart with what I have to offer. 99.99% of the time, I will get turned down. I've put that high percentage for myself, so I won't put too much hope in winning a girl's heart. I want to find out what I'm capable of doing for a girl, and going against the odds, even if it's a very tiny percentage of success.

When people say that love doesn't cost a thing, well, that's only intended for normal people. Love alone isn't enough. People don't realize that love does cost a lot; the costs aren't things that people necessarily consider. The cost that I see is physical body strength.

The cost is too much for me; it's impossible for me to obtain. People don't consider this as a cost because they don't have to worry about it, probably not even thought of. How can I experience all the wonderful experiences love has to offer? How am I able to fully show my heart to someone without that cost?

I want to win a girl's heart with my own abilities, even though it's limited due to MD. Winning a girl's heart with my own heart and from a friendship are the best ways to start a relationship, but it will be the most difficult and most painful journey.

I know that a friendship is the only chance I will have to win a girl's heart. Without being friends, a girl won't even bother to give me a look or a glance. I'll just get ignored. Chasing a girl with my heart and from friendship will have more meaning to me and with a better understanding why I chased that girl's heart. It's not going to be easy, because I will have to put in more effort and energy than anyone to win a girl's heart.

Muscular Dystrophy is too much of a burden on love. Let's say that a girl gave me a chance, she would have to give up a lot in life just to be with me. I think about the reasons that would go against me. It's her feelings that I have to consider. I can only take care of a girl's heart, her spirit, and her soul. Nice guys finish last, I guess, but then again, some just don't finish at all.

In the end, I end up losing that person. It may not be a loss at all, but it can be a blessing or a curse because someone even more deserving may come along my way. That may be true, but it's a kind of hope that I don't want.

> "There is nothing wrong in expressing your feelings to someone you love with all your heart, but you must always be sensitive to the signals and when to be rational and be attentive to her feelings. There comes a time in your life when you fall for someone who isn't interested in you because her attention is focused on someone else. There are many times when you fall in love, but the girl doesn't have the same feelings toward you." (Marisse)

There are times when Muscular Dystrophy signs say stop, but the feelings I have for a girl will persistently want me to keep trying. I know I can't do anything about that.

I had two choices: walk away or stay and keep trying, but indirectly. There is a third option, being friends. For some reason, I didn't walk away from the current girl I'm chasing now. I would have walked away if I was turned down with a heartbroken reply or an impossible answer, but instead, I was turned down gently. Sometimes being kind is just cruel. I would have walked away with a smile.

I know I should have walked away from her, but I chose the second path. There's always a possibility she will give me a chance. Sometimes I hate the part about me that won't give up on anything until the very end. Times like this, I just want to throw away that quality I have. I can't blame anyone for hurting myself; I can only blame myself for that. My kindness is hurting me.

# 6. Unseen Tears of the Heart

I fell in love with Joan. A part of me wants her to know. I know this will hurt her. Sometimes the truth is the most painful thing. I don't want to keep this secret from her anymore. This is the only secret I've kept from her.

I never thought of her as a friend or a sister, but always "The One." I saw that about her when I first met her. She brings out the best in me, but she can also close that part of me as well. I won't blame her; I never have. That's how life goes. Life isn't fair, and it's always balanced out.

I first told her how I felt and she turned me down with a gentle reply, "It's best we remain friends." I was thinking about this reply for a while, and it just hit me with my own question. Best we remain friends—best for whom, her or me? That's an easy answer: best for her. She should have broken my heart that day. If she replied, "I like you just as a friend," I would have walked away from her or just been a friend. I'll continue to chase her because I rarely get an opportunity to meet someone and feel this way toward someone. She wasn't clear about her feelings.

I am prepared to let her go, if she decides to end the relationship that she and I share. I asked her why she can't give me a chance, but she didn't answer and changed the subject. She turned it around on me instead. She said, "Peter, you have to give him a chance." After she said that, I thought to myself, that's just telling me that I will always have to give the other person the chance first. I will always be last. I was immature for asking her for an answer. I wanted to know, instead of wondering why. I backed off.

It's been a few years now, and I have only called her once or twice. I don't want my heart's feelings for her to come out over the phone and make her feel uncomfortable. Over the phone, I can't take back what is said. I used to call her often. I'm still chasing her to the point when my heart completely becomes empty. I'm trying to close that part of my heart. That's very hard to do. I've never been so lonely in my life. Seeing her is very lonesome. She asked me one time, "It must be lonely, huh?" Of course it is, but chasing love is even lonelier. I can only love her from afar.

Many people have told me that I'm on the wrong path. "Time doesn't wait. If you think you might have found the right one, treasure that person; don't let that person get away. Don't let fear hold you back. Give it a try or else you might regret later" (Unknown). If I gave up on her, then I'm an idiot for not trying. Justy Ueki Tylor said, "Just do your best and let the rest take care of itself" (*The Irresponsible Captain Tylor*). I'm seeing the path to the end. I won't put any hope that love will go my way. I will only get disappointed.

> "All speech is vain and empty unless it be accompanied by action." (Demosthenes)

She started dating someone new. My heart sank again. I thought about wanting to just walk away from her. My heart won't give up on her. I could walk away and be happy for her, or do nothing, or give her a silent good-bye, or throw away my feelings toward her, or be honorable, by giving her my love and support for the path she chose for herself. I'll let her go when she gets married. I would choose the last path when the time comes. For me to do that, I will have to give up something in return; closing a big part of my heart. As long as she's happy, I can walk away without looking back. I will be okay as long as my heart isn't fully open. When it comes down to it, her happiness is all that matters.

I don't know if meeting her was a blessing or a curse. It's probably both. I was falling endlessly; I was okay with that. I'll keep walking forward on a straight path alone with a lonely heart until a new path opens; I'll turn and see where it leads me. If it leads back to the same path, then, "Oh well;" at least I'm willing to try chasing love again. If I get turned down the first time, I won't hang around.

**Destiny**

"Destiny is not a matter of chance; it is a matter of choice" (William Jennings Bryan). I'll start over again, chasing someone's heart, but I don't know if I'll ever want to try as hard.

I believe that no one is born with a destiny. Destiny isn't going to come knocking on my doorstep. I have to make my own sense of my destiny. It doesn't always seem to make sense. Finding my own destiny is one of many journeys in life; I just have to take the first step and walk forward. The only person stopping me is me. This journey isn't easy. There is hardship and pain along the way. Some people accept their destiny given by birth; some have their destiny in mind; some go out and find theirs; some try to change theirs; some aren't destined to do anything.

Mera Ing, a friend, said this to me, "Some people are destined to be in pain." Why would anyone want to live life being in pain (physical and emotional) all the time? No one wants that, and definitely no one would ask to be born with that destiny. Maybe I'm destined to be in pain, and carrying heavier burdens than anyone else. I try to live my life to the utmost with a very lonely heart. I'm also destined to help others by giving others hope and to give inspiration to others (normal and disabled individuals) with my struggles.

Without pain, I wouldn't feel alive. I would just be an empty shell, waiting for death to come knocking on my door. I want to help others with the pain I go through in life, so that others may have a good idea of why their lives can easily be taken for granted. I see that as my destiny, but I don't want to be in pain the rest of my life. My destiny can't be altered, and yet I am trying to change my destiny. I am taking a step forward each day. That's all I can do.

> Everyone has a part of themselves they don't like. You carry it around like a weight. The lucky ones realize that when it becomes too heavy, you can choose to set it down. That's when you see things the way they really are. ("Night Without Stars")

I know everyone has secrets they hide from others, because truth doesn't always bring happiness. I know the heart can't falsify the truths that it bears.

Love can either be the greatest feeling or the greatest pain in the universe. "Love is big. It's a bright light in the universe. And a bright light casts a big shadow" ("Romancing the Joan"). The stronger the feelings are, the stronger the pain becomes.

That night I went to bed trying to let all my tears out, but my tears weren't falling. "Tears may be dried up, but the heart— never" (Margerite Gardiner). I had so many thoughts going through my mind, good things and bad things.

> "We all carry around so much pain in our hearts. Love and pain and beauty. They all seem to go together like one little tidy confusing package. It's a messy business, life. It's hard to figure—full of surprises. Some good. Some bad." (Henry Bromel)

I was right to keep the advice I would give to someone with MD: "Don't fall in love."

Ashly is right to say that, "Love is what keeps you going in life," and "Love is your kind of hope in life." I chose love for that kind of strength to keep going.

Sometimes, pain needs to be let out from the heart because it can become so heavy. We can't deal with it alone. I'm just like everyone else. Everyone needs support from others. Why did I allow myself and my heart to get hurt this much from love?

"Love will enter cloaked in friendship's name" (Ovid). If I knew that, why didn't I stop myself?

"To be brave is to love someone unconditionally, without expecting anything in return. To just give. That takes courage, because we don't want to fall on our faces or leave ourselves open to hurt." (Madonna)

"It hurts because you feel it because you're alive. You love people. That generates a lot of power, a lot of energy, same kind of energy that binds atoms together. And we've all seen what happens when you try to pry them apart . . . It's in your nature to get attached to people. I put that in the recipe. It's when you guys try to ignore that, when you try to go at it alone, that's when it gets ugly. It's hell." ("Death Be Not Whatever")

"I love life . . . Yeah, I'm sad, but at the same time, I'm really happy that something could make me feel that sad. It's like, it makes me feel alive, you know. It makes me feel human. The only way I could feel this sad now is if I felt something really good before. So I have to take the bad with the good. So I guess what I'm feeling is like a beautiful sadness." ("Raisins")

My burdens and loneliness are becoming heavier and heavier. It's not that I have someone to share my burdens with me, so I have to endure them alone. "Everyone is crossing a bridge with more weight than they can bear. So you juggle." ("Friday Night")

I know from experience that I will always have to take the initiative with anything, not just with love. When I do stop taking the initiative on chasing love, nothing will happen. I won't have anything to do with love. "Love is the fundamental ingredient for everything" (Loreman). Everything has to do with love one way or another. Everyone needs love. Without that kind of love in our hearts, our real self, our character, will not be able to show itself. Character is portrayed from the whole heart and not from bits and pieces of the heart.

On *Joan of Arcadia,* "Only Connect," Joan was asked the question, "Do you miss yourself?" I asked myself that question because I know that I am changing, shutting down my emotions. The more I try to fight this change, the faster I change. I have always been able to fight this kind of change from the inside, but that change would make life easier and without pain from everything, from physical limitations to love. Change is something no one can escape or fight.

"Change has a considerable psychological impact on the human mind. To the fearful it is threatening because it means that things may get worse. To the hopeful it is encouraging because things may get better. To the confident it is inspiring because the challenge exists to make things better." (King Whitney Jr.)

Change is bound to happen sooner or later. Change is a part of life.

I do miss my old self. I was optimistic, talkative, enjoyed life more (listening to music and watching movies), having a better outlook on life (positive thinking), interested in other people's lives, and didn't have a mask on. I know I can't hide this change from others.

I have always believed that if I were to be like Jason, life would be so much easier than actually being the person I am now. I wouldn't have to worry about anything, keeping my feelings hidden from others, not wanting to make friends, having a negative outlook on things, playing games all day, not taking care of my health, and most of all, not trying to chase after love.

Jason said this about Joan and me; "You and Joan are being mean to each other in a 'nice' way." The TV was on one day and it was about a girl who had been friends with a guy for a year, and she gave him an ultimatum. He had to decide to leave his current girlfriend for her, or the friendship would be over. In the end, he chose her. She got a happy ending, but a sad ending for the other girl. After we saw that, Jason wants me to do that to Joan. I told him I can't do that to her. That's all I said to him, and he called me a "big idiot." Even if I did that, I know I'll get the short end of the stick. Knowing Joan, she would definitely end our relationship that we share. Jason asked, "You want me to do that to her for you?" I said, "No." Then he said, "Fine, be in pain and sad all the time! You're a loser." I know he means well, and that he's looking out for me. He gave a name to my situation: The Joan Syndrome.

I have thought about Joan's feelings on this too. I asked her, "Do I sense that you do have feelings toward me?" Joan did not deny it. The 'why' part I feel from her is that she is scared of how her life will be with me. How much of her normal life would change? How much of her life she would have to give up? She has her whole life ahead of her. If she tells me that, then I would understand and stop chasing her.

Kindness can only go so far and, in this situation, kindness can be so cruel. It'll hurt more than the truth. Really, kindness has nothing to do with this situation. That's why I said, "Joan broke my heart with her kindness." I mean it.

> "The actions that you decided to take were never useless. The many things you have done; the many people you have met; they are all stars that make up the universe called 'you.' They are all stars to you. There are no useless stars." ("Our Star, the Leaf Star")

What am I going to do with all these strong feelings for Joan? I can't give them back to her; she definitely can't take them back. My heart just can't let them go or throw them away that easily.

Will I attend Joan's wedding? Most likely not. I don't want Joan to hope or expect anything from me. I know Joan will be very disappointed and hurt by my decision. I also don't want to have that memory of Joan getting wed because I won't be able to forget her image. That would be torture to my heart. It's like walking away from Joan's life in a silent way and as a silent goodbye. I would tell Joan, "Live the life that I can't have, or share with you to the fullest—no matter how I'm feeling. All that matters most are your feelings, not mine." I'll accept that Joan wants a normal life and not a life with MD. The decisions she's made will lead her heart in the direction of a normal life, where her heart resides.

Here's a suggestion from David:

> You are torturing yourself. You have given Joan so much power over your heart and soul; I know she

doesn't know that she has this power over you. You will not find peace by walking away, your heart and soul will continue to torture you. You may try to lock it away in that box in your head, like you have many things locked up, but they nibble at your soul and you carry that burden.

You wouldn't dishonor your mother or father, so don't dishonor yourself. It sucks to sit in your chair and NOT be able to effect that which you want . . . to not have the power to get to where you want to be, where your heart and soul want you to be: with Joan. By accepting that, by honoring Joan with your love and support, you will unburden your heart of many things; and you will continue to be a part of something beautiful.

When Jason and I were going to Ashly's house for the first time for dinner, Ashly gave me a heads-up about Joan inviting her boyfriend to dinner. Joan kind of forced that on me. She knows that I can't handle that. I felt that Joan took my heart for granted. That really hurt me, and I couldn't answer Ashly. I just froze for a minute. I thought it would be an easy day, but it was going to be a difficult one. Jason spoke out and said, "So you're not going, right?" Ashly looked at me with a shocked expression and said, "You're not going!?" I couldn't answer her right away because my heart was still handling the pain of hearing that. I did tell Ashly, "I will go, not for Joan but for you." I made that decision to go because of how disappointed Ashly would have been if I didn't go.

My heart was calm when Joan and Ashly came over to pick us up. Ashly being there kept my heart calm. I didn't let them see my pain. I wouldn't ruin that day for Ashly and Jason. It's not my place to do so. Jason was looking forward to seeing her house.

We were at the store buying groceries before going to Ashly's house. She went out to buy the stuff while Joan stayed in the car with us. She wanted to know what's happening in my life. I really couldn't answer her directly. I didn't say much to her. I wanted to tell her everything, but my heart wasn't there with me. I told her things that I could tell her, but it's only a small percent of the whole. I didn't want to accidentally say something that was not meant for her to know. My heart was thinking about her the whole time.

Ashly's house was small but nice and cozy. I was helping Joan and Ashly in the kitchen while Jason was playing video games with Ashly's husband. I really didn't talk to Joan. I was keeping my heart calm around her. Ashly's presence also helped keep my heart calm. I talked to Ashly about being calm when Joan went to set the dinner table. Joan came back in the kitchen to get napkins and stuff, and she said, "I'm really happy that you came to meet him," referring to her boyfriend. I didn't say anything back to her. It was hard on me when she said that. How can she possibly believe that I came to meet her boyfriend? I know that I can turn this around on myself by saying, "I have to consider her feelings as well." It has to be one or the other and not both. If it's both, then it will be an impossible situation because nothing will happen. Everyone is selfish, one way or another. I'm selfish too. I wouldn't meet him if it wasn't for Ashly and Jason.

I endured for them. I wouldn't do anything to hurt them. It's not their fault, but it's between Joan and me. I was calm the whole time before dinner. I was being myself and talking a lot.

When Joan's boyfriend showed up, I took a deep breath to keep my heart from being unstable. I've told myself that I wouldn't pay attention to their relationship or to their conversations. I was nice and polite to him. What else could I have done? Ashly once said to me, "You're nice to others, but you're nicer to us than you are to others." I do notice that. I was sitting next to Joan like always. I kept calm the whole time. I wasn't acting my usual self. I stopped talking like I usually do. I only talked a bit. I was like that the rest of the night. Ashly thought I might have been even worse than I was.

After dinner, Joan and Ashly handed out presents for Jason and me. I gave them a card with advice about family and time. That's the only thing I can give them. I didn't want any presents because there's nothing I want. The only thing I want is the one thing only Joan can give me: being in a relationship with her. I told Ashly, "There's nothing I want that you can give me. All I want was Joan. You can't give me her, only Joan."

I wrote this for them:

Time

Some see time as a blessing; some see it as being cruel; some see it as a gift; some see it as being unfair. With all these perspectives of time, it doesn't matter because time will not rewind, nor will time stop, but rather time will always move forward. Time waits for no one. Time does not discriminate; no matter who it is.

"Time is the coin of your life. It is the only coin you have, and only you can determine how it will be spent. Be careful lest you let other people spend it for you." (Carl Sandburg)

Time can cause anything without restrictions. Time can cause doubts, pains, regrets, and so on. Time can also cause others to push people away. Some spend all their time on a career; some spend all their time with God; some spend all their time on helping others; some spend all their time on school; some spend all their time with friends. Now-a-days, people don't have time for family: parents and siblings. People can spend all their time on things that will always be there, but their parents and siblings won't.

"Time only seems to matter when it's running out." (Peter Strup)

Set aside time for your family regularly by calling, emailing, writing a letter, or visiting. We don't know when our time will end.

"Know the true value of time; snatch, seize, and enjoy every moment of it. No idleness; no laziness; no procrastination; never put off till tomorrow what you can do today." (Phillip Stanhope, 4th Earl of Chesterfield)

Remember, time can cause regrets. Once your time is gone, God will not give you more, and certainly, God will not give your time back. Which perspectives of time will you perceive? How will you use time?

"Be wise in the use of time. The question in life is not 'how much time do we have?' The question is 'what shall we do with it?'" (Anna Robertson Brown Lindsay)

Then I told them why I wrote it. I care about them very much. I was listening to each of them very carefully because they might say something about each other, something like being very busy and not having time for each other. Joan said she was very busy, and Ashly said she hasn't heard from Joan in over a month. I don't want them to lose their close, sisterhood bond they have with one another. Joan was happy afterward. She gave me a smile. Then we watched an episode of *Joan of Arcadia*, "Friday Night." It was a sad episode with a lot of meaning. I taped it for them to see because I wanted to show them what I learned from it. I wasn't watching the show because I had seen it a few times. Joan wasn't sitting with me though.

Afterward, we had dessert. Joan said, "He was really impressed with you two." My heart was becoming a bit unstable by now. I stopped myself from saying, "Joan, I didn't come here today to impress your boyfriend. I didn't even want to come. I only came because it would mean a lot to Ashly if I came to see her house. That's all."

Then Joan just sat there with this look on her face. I can tell in her eyes that she wanted me to talk to her about what I've been doing or asking her what she's been doing. I couldn't ask her or tell her. My feelings for her and my pains from her created a very high and very thick wall in my heart which only comes up around Joan, even if Ashly is there. I sense that Joan noticed that from me, that I haven't been able to talk to her for a long time. When she got up to get a cup of tea, I tilted my head back, looked up, took a deep breath, and exhaled. This helps to calm my heart.

Then Joan and Ashly decided to take us home. Joan took Jason and wheeled him over to the car because he always goes in first. I went with Ashly. She asked me if my neck was tired. I said to myself, "What's she talking about?" Then I realized why she said that. I didn't know that Ashly was observing my behavior when I tilted my head back to calm my heart. I did that again. I looked up, took a deep breath, released, and said, "Not yet. Not yet." I wasn't able to keep my heart calm any longer.

Ashly 's husband and Joan's boyfriend came as well. Joan sat in the back with me. She wanted to. I didn't talk much to Joan in the car. She asked me if I was going to write her an email the next day. I was thinking to myself, "Why would she ask me that?" I asked her if she wanted me to. She said, "Yes," with a smile. She didn't tell me why she wanted me to write to her. I knew what she wanted me to talk about. I did write to her the next day, but I didn't talk about what I felt Joan wanted me to write about. I felt that she wanted me to tell her what I thought about her boyfriend. She didn't say that directly to me. If she did, then she's taking my heart for granted or she's being inconsiderate of my feelings. I wrote, "I feel that I know what you want me to talk about on this email, but I'm sorry, Joan. I won't say anything."

Then Joan asked me to get a camera to take a picture of everyone to keep as a memory of our day out. I only looked at the photo once, when I was sending it to Joan and Ashly. After I sent it, I deleted it. Jason said, "Joan picked him over you." "What did Joan do to my brother? He's all messed up." "Just give it up." "You two shouldn't be friends anymore." "You should burn up everything that reminds you of Joan." What I learned from all this is that I'm just as selfish as everyone else. Every selfless decision that I come up with, I end up seeing them with a little bit of selfishness in them. "Every instance of heartbreak can teach us powerful lessons about creating the kind of love we really want" (Martha Beck). Every decision has a selfish side to it. It doesn't matter. The human heart is selfish. No one can say that they're not selfish.

Gentleness and kindness leads to swaying feelings and truths.

> "Life can only be understood backwards; but it must be lived forwards." (Soren Kierkegaard)

> "Life is an escalator: You can move forward or backward; you cannot remain still." (Patricia Russell-McCloud)

> "To look backward for a while is to refresh the eye, to restore it, and to render it the more fit for its prime function of looking forward." (Margaret Fairless Barber)

**End to Beginning**

Then I found out she got engaged.

**End**

When Ashly came over for lunch, and she told me that Joan was engaged, my heart just collapsed. I couldn't respond or say anything. I've been preparing my heart for this pain for a long time that Joan would eventually get engaged. No matter how much I've anticipated and prepared for it, it didn't do any good. My heart was devastated from the false hope she gave me. How was I supposed to feel after hearing that? The pain was so intense that I couldn't contain it to myself. I couldn't handle it. I couldn't cry because I wasn't sad. I was just really hurt. It was horrible.

Afterward, I went in my room and just stared at the computer screen. I just collapsed from the pain. I tried to let it all out, but couldn't. I'm not strong enough to cry. Then Joan called and said she was in the neighborhood and wanted to stop by to visit. When she drove by, I took a deep breath to try to calm down the pain in my heart, but it didn't help me at all. I was calm enough to see her. I couldn't look at her engagement ring. Worst of all, I couldn't say, "Congratulations," to her. I may never be able to say it.

She mentioned her engagement. I couldn't say anything and I just sat there looking at her. I couldn't answer her. She looked in my eyes and asked me, "Are you sad?" I didn't answer her. Then she asked another question, "What are you feeling?" I finally answered her. I told her, "I'm not sad, just really hurt." She was puzzled and asked me, "Hurt, why?" I didn't answer her.

Joan looks so happy—more so than I've ever seen her. Why can't I just be happy for her? I felt the greatest sadness in my heart because I wasn't the one she picked to give her that happiness. I couldn't compete for her. How could I? I can't compete with someone who can physically do things with her. When did the chair or MD come in, at the beginning or at the end? She had the opportunity to see past the chair or MD. Ashly said that to me. Joan could have proven my thinking about relationships wrong. I couldn't win her heart. I really tried with everything that I have and that's my heart. I had nothing else to chase her with. I've put in more effort and energy than anyone.

I'm not going to chase after love anymore or make any more friends. There's no point. I don't want to let my heart hurt itself anymore. I don't want to have this feeling again. Even if I did chase after love again, I won't be nice about it. I mean I won't take a gentle response if she doesn't have feelings for me. I will get her to give me an honest answer. If not, I'm not going to stick around. Even if she does give an honest answer, I'm still going to walk away. I'm not going to waste my time. It doesn't matter what kind of connection or how much we have in common with one another when I'm considered "just a friend." What's the point? Time is what they won't have. My heart is exhausted; it's just out of energy to even bother trying again. Love discriminates; hate doesn't. I won't bother trying to prove myself wrong on life or relationships.

Mrs. Schneider said, "You always take the most difficult paths in life, and never the easy ones."

# 7. Waterfalls

I did write a wedding scenario called "Waterfalls." It was written as a screenplay, less action but a lot of emotions. I know it's not an accurate screenplay; I wrote it as if I went to her wedding reception and was finally able to tell her what I really feel inside. I decided to finish it because I feel that Joan needs a reason why I won't attend her wedding. I've also written it to get it all out in the open for myself. I know my heart became stronger for having written it, but I don't feel my heart being any stronger, just very empty. This is a way for me to move on. My advice for myself was to go beyond the pain. In real life, no one speaks proper English or with any language.

I named the wedding scenario "Waterfalls" based on the word "falls." Everyone's life is like a river. It never stops moving and always in one direction: forward. We all come to waterfalls (difficulties, pains, suffering, and trials) at any given time. Waterfalls lead us to hit rock bottom. The river doesn't stop or dry up. It simply keeps moving forward until another and another waterfall comes our way. It never ends.

I'm not running anymore because I'm at the end of the road. "The world is round and the place which may seem like the end may also be the beginning" (Ivy Baker Priest). The end of the road can be an end or a beginning, or both, for us.

"You gain strength, courage and confidence by every experience in which you really stop to look fear in the face. You are able to say to yourself, 'I have lived through this horror. I can take the next thing that comes along.' You must do the thing you think you cannot do." (Eleanor Roosevelt)

"The moment we find the reason behind an emotion . . . the wall we have built is breached, and the positive memories it has kept from us return too. That's why it pays to ask those painful questions. The answers can set you free." (Gloria Steinem)

I will stay in Joan's life but I won't attend her wedding. She asked me to but I still didn't change my mind. My heart isn't strong enough. If there was another word that is heavier than "devastated," that's how I would feel if I attended. I wish that my heart was strong enough to be able to attend. Taking this path, I will be able to save my heart and not change completely. I'll stay in her life to create something beautiful and special with her even though it's not the kind of love I want with her.

"We don't accomplish anything in this world alone . . . and whatever happens is the result of the whole tapestry of one's life and all the weavings of individual threads from one to another that creates something." (Sandra Day O'Connor)

I don't regret meeting Joan, but rather I'm thankful I met her. "Gratitude is our most direct line to God and the angels. If we take the time, no matter how crazy and troubled we feel, we can find something to be thankful for" (Terry Lynn Taylor).

I'm grateful to Joan for all the little things she has done for me. "Be thankful for the least gift, so shalt thou be meant to receive greater" (Thomas á Kempis). She changed my character and heart so much to where it is now. I was able to experience all the emotions of the human heart. "Let us be grateful to people who make us happy: They are the charming gardeners who make our souls blossom" (Marcel Proust). I felt the dark emotions of the heart: anger, bitterness, devastation, disappointment, envy, expectation, false hope, frustration, heartbreak, pain, resentment, sadness, suffering, and so on. I have also felt the light emotions of the heart: calmness, forgiveness, happiness, hope, joy, love, patience, peace, and so on. I was able to make beautiful, encouraging, fun, joyful, hopeful, happy, laughing, painful, sad, strengthening, tearful, and wonderful memories with her. "Feeling grateful to or appreciative of someone or something in your life actually attracts more of the things that you appreciate and value into your life" (Christiane Northrup, M.D.). Those memories are my treasures. My heart values these memories more than anything.

I was motivated to do some good things and to share my heart with others. I was able to meet a few very wonderful people, who became close friends, and a part of my family that I choose. "The bond that links your true family is not one of blood, but of respect and joy in each other's life. Rarely do members of one family grow up under the same roof" (Richard Bach).

My heart is in a state that doesn't expect anything from anyone, but I'm always doing things with an optimistic attitude. I can give up at any time. The false hope Joan gave me literally killed my heart. It wasn't right; it wasn't wrong;

and definitely, it wasn't fair. I don't know how my heart is doing or saying anymore. My heart is staggering back and forth: giving up or not giving up. My heart is empty, and it's not empty; the pain is there, and it's not there; it's okay, and it's not okay; it doesn't care, and it does care; it's sad, and it's not sad; it's shattered, and it's not shattered; it's open, and it's not open. My heart feels empty and wants to give up or shut down because, "With only obstinacy to support your heart, you never know when you'll just flitter away" ("With a little prayer").

David Erickson sees how I portrayed my heart now with a different perspective than mine. He sees the state of my heart in this way:

Your heart is the same today as it ever was. You must go beyond your mind to your soul; only there can you get back to YOU. We sometimes become our environments . . . it takes work to go beyond the world and get deep into our souls; for there, we live in peace. You must try. Your pain comes from worldly human conditions; not from your heart. Only your mind is broken—not your heart and soul–and you CAN find your way back. Reading books is good; praying is good; thinking is good; being silent is good. You've lost your connection with your soul. Pray, to whomever you find comfort; only with silence can you find your inner voice of freedom. I know that the "world" has ripped you off, both with your health and with your lost love, but down inside your soul is peace. Find it.

I will try and find my way back to my soul, to be able to hear the voice of my heart again. I have to find a reason that will build that bridge that connects my heart and soul together.

Making a big difference in people's lives and touching their hearts is my reason. I was able to pass my heart on to theirs, making them better human beings. Then they will be able to pass my heart and theirs onto others they meet. "The life I touch for good or ill will touch another life, and that in turn another, until who knows where the trembling stops or in what far place my touch will be felt" (Frederick Buechner).

## Joan's Wedding Day

This is a special and happiest day of Joan's life, her wedding. On the other hand, this day is the most painful and saddest day of my life. I end up not attending, even knowing that being there would matter to her. I just couldn't go. It's so painful for me just thinking about it. I wouldn't be able to look toward Joan the whole time. And I wouldn't be able to hide my pain and sadness from anyone. I won't kid myself about that. I regret not attending. I am 95% consumed by all this because I allowed it. I wanted to stay in bed, so that I can cry to get all my tears out.

> "He has to stop wanting to cry and get stronger. So that he'll be able to go on without crying, no matter what. But you also need the strength to be able to cry when you want to." (*Tsubasa Chronicle*)

I tried to cry the night before, but I couldn't, nor did my tears fall. "If you don't cry when you want to, you are not going to smile" (*Mahou Sensei Negima*). I'm trying so hard to let them

85

fall, but nothing happens. I was never able to cry about it. My heart is completely broken or empty or completely dead. I don't feel anything from my heart. I know I'm sad, hurt and angry, but I don't feel anything.

## Prolonging Life

If I've lost everything, why would I want to prolong my life? I have thought about the question Joan and Ashly had asked me. "Why do you say all this, that you don't enjoy anything, don't want anything, don't expect anything from anyone, stopped being interested in things, don't want to do anything, and all that; and yet why do you want to prolong your life by going on a ventilator?" Honestly, I can't really answer that. I know how to answer it, but they won't like it. The best way for me to answer is by clearly explaining the reason that I am contradicting everything and for me to go on the ventilator when the time comes.

I remembered what I had said to Dr. Clark at one of my Muscular Dystrophy Association clinics. We were discussing if Jason or I needed antidepressant pills. Dr. Clark can tell that I don't need it because I'm okay about my life. What I said to Dr. Clark was that there will be a time in my life that I would become balanced—emotionally balanced—where my thinking will be right in the middle—neither positive nor negative. Being like that, I'll become empty. Another term for it is called "being dead" because I wouldn't be doing anything. I wouldn't enjoy, laugh, smile, cry, sad, angry, upset, at anything. I stop living. I wonder why I had said that all those years ago. I didn't know how, what, when, who, and why that would get me to be like that. I'm almost at that stage, but there are reasons preventing me from being completely like that.

I'm sure I won't get to that path, but in time, a path may open up again.

My feelings and thoughts were based on a lie, or a mistake, or a misunderstanding, or an uncertainty. I have to think that it was a good thing. I stopped being naïve about life. My character, feelings, heart, and thoughts are changed from it. I don't like it, but I don't hate who I've become from my sad experiences. I can't rewind the clock; I can't go backward; I can only take a step forward each day with the "me" of today.

I did expect a lot from others, but now I don't expect much or anything from anyone. This is something I have learned to believe. It was my fault to expect a lot from others because I set a very high expectation on myself. I still have that set even now. I do more for others than I should have. I do understand why it is the way it is. I'm not disappointed or hurt by others after I stopped expecting a lot from others.

My thinking has changed. I don't want much in this world because MD took a lot away from me and is still going to take a lot more. I'm forcing myself to think that I can't have anything I really want, no matter how hard I try to obtain them. I had always fallen short in whatever I really wanted to do or to have. It's not something new to me, but I keep trying and trying, knowing that I'm just going to fall short. My thought on this has changed from "nothing is impossible" to "nothing is possible." I can put it this way: Anything is possible if, and only if, it's within your own limitations, physical or emotional. I don't want to kid myself anymore that I can have anything I really want with hard work, being persistent, determination, trying, being positive, believing in myself, wishing, hoping, praying, and all that jazz. But still, a small part of me will instinctively try.

This way of thinking will keep me grounded with the reality of living with MD and not getting ahead of my own limitations, physical and emotional. The things that I really want are beyond my limitations and also world limitations. World limitations for me are looks, walking, transportation, independence from others, and society's standards. Most people don't even consider these as limitations.

I was asked, "Why don't you want to nominate yourself or make a wish on the show 'Three Wishes'?" I can't rely on wishes. Wishes are granted by other people who are able to go past the person's (who is making the wish) own limitations. And my one wish goes beyond everyone's limitations. I can only make wishes that are under the boundaries of human limitations. It's who I am that won't allow me to wish for anything for myself. I believe that making wishes and getting them granted makes a person spoiled and rely on them too much. But people need to have wishes because it gives them a bit of hope. If a wish came true for me, I wouldn't feel anything because I didn't deserve it and haven't earned it by myself. I believe in working hard and being determined to get what you want in life. I can't wish to have fewer responsibilities because I have a lot of them, and they're all within my limitations. There's nothing I really want to make a wish for. I can't believe in wishes because they cause favoritism. Why is one wish granted and not the other? Who decides what wishes are granted and for whom? They're too unfair.

I'm not fighting it; I am changing, and I'm not doing anything about it. I'm not even trying to prevent it from consuming me. I'm just continuing to let time take its course to whatever becomes of me. Am I trying to be strong about it? No, I force myself to be this strong all the time. I know it's okay to be weak sometimes.

I continue to be strong so I am able to do things. It's harder because I used love, as in romance, as a base for being strong. I chased that kind of love with everything I had because it makes me the strongest. Why not base that with other kinds of love, like from family or friends? Well, for one, it doesn't allow me to reach my highest potential because there's a limit on how far I can use that type of love. I can't completely use my heart. There is pressure and expectations from people to maintain the same level of strength all the time. My mom put a lot of expectation on me and no one else. When will there be a time when I can be strong for myself and not for others? There isn't, because it doesn't work like that.

Maybe contradicting everything helps me deal with all this. I don't know who is real, my realistic thinking or my open minded thinking. I'm not even picking which side to take. I'll accept both sides of who I am. Life is about contradictions. "If you accept that they both can exist simultaneously, then you can find peace in the contradictions" ("The Rise and Fall of Joan Girardi").

Maybe I'm living longer to give as much of my love to my loved ones, pass on as much of my heart, and create as many memories for everyone. Other people's love for me is keeping me from becoming completely emotionally balanced and for me to prolong my life. I have to be "the me of today" for others because I know the impact I have on them.

If there's even a tiny light in me (the will or spirit or a reason, even if it isn't a reason of my choice), I want to keep going. If one person still needs me, then I will use that as a stepping stone to continue to keep taking a step forward. It's easier not to go on the ventilator and not prolong my life, but what would that do? It would make it easier on my mom and my family; one less person or burden to take care of. This is who I am. If I wasn't, I would have given up already. I clearly see the effects on people, even the effects I don't see, but the effects are happening.

> "You are MUCH more aware of yourself at levels WAY deeper than others ever dreamed of . . . and THAT is what will keep you with us, my friend. Only lie down for the last time when you are ready; until then, keep fighting. You have lots to offer the collective world, and you care about the fight." (David Erickson)

I'm going to prolong my life for others, not for my sake. It's not like I'm that miserable, sad, or suffering from life with Muscular Dystrophy. I'm smart enough not to hurt myself from everything from MD. I'm not depressed, but the pain is there. I have accepted the pain. As one of my friends said, "That's just who you are."

# 8. A Fading Breath

After all this heartbreak, my respiratory became difficult. I can still remember how I used to breathe, with a subtle inhale of breath and with ease. I was breathing like that for a good while. There was no drastic change through all those years. Changes should have caught up with me during those years. I don't know the reasons why my respiration didn't change. It's kind of like the "mind over matter" concept, but "mind over health."

When my respiratory system took a nose dive, it changed drastically. I wasn't prepared for this change to happen instantly, nor were my doctors. When I breathe, I have to use all my neck muscles. I breathe like a fish out of water.

I went to see my pulmonologist and to get a lung function test every three to four months. Before, it was only twice a year. My test numbers were always dropping little by little, but not much. Now the tests results are so low that on paper I have no lung functions.

My respiratory doctor recommended that I use a BiPAP (Bilevel Positive Airway Pressure) machine at night to give my diaphragm a rest from all the heavy breathing during the day. He wanted me to use it to get used to it. When I started using it at night, I didn't like it one bit. I didn't like the nasal mask. It makes my skin irritated and causes redness. Most of the time, air would leak out the sides of the mask. It's annoying to sleep with that condition. The sensation of air blowing in my nose constantly to fill up my lungs felt weird. For the first time, I felt claustrophobic. It took a week to get used to it.

After a while, my lungs had gotten weaker from using the BiPAP because it causes dependency. I noticed a huge difference in my breathing. My breathing became heavier than before. It tired me out fast. For the first time, I felt what it was like to suffocate. It's a horrible feeling. I'm always catching my breath constantly. I'm lightly coughing all day.

Most of the time, my nose gets congested while sleeping. I wake up finding myself not able to breathe with the nasal mask. The scary part is that I can't pull off the mask. I'm saying to myself, "Where's the air?" So I breathe with my mouth open, but I don't inhale enough air in my lungs. I feel like gasping for air. Eventually my nose clears up a bit, which allows me to breathe with the BiPAP. I feel relieved when that happens. I've been having more nightmares than before due to lack of oxygen. I find myself waking up with horrible dry mouth each morning. It's a disgusting feeling.

Using the restroom after I wake up is the most difficult time of the day to breathe. I use the toilet and I feel that I'm suffocating because I have to hold my breath to push. Taking a shower is just as difficult to do because of the water, mist and steam. I can't enjoy a hot shower anymore. The worst part is brushing my teeth. I'm really fighting for air when brushing. It's so horrible. I quickly finish just to get out of the restroom.

If I add in eating along with breathing, that's tough. Chewing and breathing together is tiresome. I end up struggling to finish my meal. I end up not eating enough because I lose my appetite after a few bites. I dread eating.

Talking and breathing is a good and bad situation. I'm still going to talk regardless. If I have to pause for a breath halfway through the sentence, I will. People do notice that from me and say, "Stop talking. Save your breath." I respond with a no. Sometimes, I have to repeat myself because family and friends can't hear me. I would comment: "Stop making me repeat myself; I'm running out of air, you know." Then we all just laugh.

The weather also plays a big role with my breathing difficulties. Very hot days are very tough and miserable. I fight to get enough air in my lungs with each breath. My lungs and my neck muscles wear me out by just breathing. When it's nice and cool, I only have a short period of difficulty breathing, and that is around the middle of the evening.

Being in the van to go places is difficult for me to breathe. It's hot, stuffy, and small in there. I feel anxious and nauseated in the van. I have the air conditioner on to help me breathe easier. I just can't wait to get out of the van. Being away from my BiPAP is difficult because I would have to tough it out when my breathing becomes very difficult. I don't want to worry the people I'm going out with. I try to hide that fact when I'm out.

I know I can use my BiPAP during the day, but I have to be stuck in bed. That is so boring. It is also a hassle to get on and off the bed. Every night, I couldn't wait go to bed because the

BiPAP is there waiting for me. That's the best time of day because I won't have to fight too hard for a breath. Thank goodness I have my BiPAP by my bed. The first breath I take from it is so relieving.

My quality of life decreased so much from respiratory difficulties. I'll have to get a tracheotomy, which I do not want. It's horrible hearing stories about having it. You can't talk; you can't eat; stuck in bed forever. If there's a way to breathe without getting the tracheotomy, I will go for it. I didn't expect having difficulty breathing would be a pain in the ass, but as long as I can laugh about it, I can handle it. Life without air is what I live with.

**Moon Over Water**

I imagine the moon symbolizing all my health issues, hanging above me as I struggle to stay afloat. I have asked myself this question: How do I really feel about all these health changes? I'm okay with it. They're just more hassles to take care of, with more appointments, equipment and suffering. I already have a full plate and an extra plate wouldn't make a difference.

I don't have anyone to run to, cry to, lean on, confide in (my heart, sadness, pains, tears, worries, and fears), and to get comfort from. I can't put everything on someone. I can't do that with family or friends.

I've dealt with everything on my own emotionally—my health, and all the things that I can do without any help. I wouldn't ask for help knowing that I can do it myself. I'm reluctant to ask because I don't want to rely on anyone. It's been like that for a long time. It was hard, lonely and scary.

Everything changed. My heart and emotional state changed greatly, and all my health changes starting to progress further. I became really scared of my emotional changes, from my reasoning, thoughts and understanding on life.

I'm not scared of getting a ventilator. I am scared of how I'm breathing now. I hate it, and it's very scary to handle. I don't know how long my breathing will stay this way. It can go out tonight when I'm sleeping, tomorrow, in a week, a month, or a year. I can't tell how long I have. And that's scary not knowing.

I'm scared of falling off from the weight I carry. I don't have someone who will catch me. It's scary going through life alone. I'm scared that one day I will give up because I lost the strength and the will that I had that kept me from falling. Everyone sees me doing better because I'm creating good memories for them. Death scares me the most because of my loved ones. I won't be able to see or talk to my loved ones anymore. All these health changes are bringing me closer to that time.

At my deathbed, I hope that my loved ones will be there for my passing. What I hope from my mom is that she'll be there with me while holding my hand and looking in my eyes and say, "Peter, you did good." Then she gives me a gentle kiss. Then I'll say, "See you in a bit." Then I say, "I love you, mom." And she says, "I love you too." Then I pass away with a smile. "When somebody dies, you only part for a short while. If we live to our fullest, we'll meet in heaven. Shake their hand farewell for now. It's only for a while. A little while" (Major TV). I hate goodbyes. I would also want to be cremated, so that everyone can say "goodbye" in their own way. Any way they feel comfortable doing: pouring my ashes over a waterfall, river or ocean; sailing my ashes on a paper boat on a river or ocean; letting the wind carry my ashes away; or whatever.

A few months later my breathing became worse.

## Pneumonia

One day I felt sick. I had a headache, fever, a light cough, and was congested. I was in bed on the BiPAP. It was a little harder to breathe. I woke up and used the bathroom. Breathing was harder that morning. I was coughing and gasping for air. I had just enough energy to breathe and be able to use the toilet, but then I panicked after ten minutes. I was out of breath. With the last of my energy, I called out to my mom that I was done. "What's wrong?" she asked in Chinese. "Mom, I can't breathe. No air," I said with a distressed look. She hurried up and got me done. Mom put me in my wheelchair, and I hurried into my room. Mom was right behind me. I parked abruptly in the middle of the room. Mom almost ran into me. She quickly picked me up and put me on my bed. I was panting while mom turned on the BiPAP. She quickly grabbed the tube and nasal mask and put it on me in five seconds. I got the first breath and felt relieved. I was on the BiPAP the whole morning. I could breathe. When lunchtime came, I figured I could go off the BiPAP for lunch. I went off the BiPAP for a few minutes and suddenly I was gasping for air.

"Again?" I said with angry tone. My diaphragm felt very tired. I was hoping that I wasn't dependent on it. Figured it was just a bad day. "What now?" Mom said softly and scared. "I can't do it," I said, looking away from mom. "You can't what?" she said. "I need air, Mom." I said quickly as I was rolled toward my room. Mom ran quickly to my room and hooked me up to the BiPAP. I wasn't in bed. I was still in my wheelchair. That way I could watch television. Mom went out and came back with my lunch. I had a hard time eating with the BiPAP on. I ate a little bit of my lunch. "Eat a little more." She said. "I can't, Mom. Too hard," I said abruptly. Mom asked me to drink a can of Ensure (a nutritional shake). I did. "I'll be back later. Are you okay for now?" she asked. I nodded. She left for work like she always does. I stayed on the BiPAP all day. I didn't want to go through that feeling again. Dinner came along and the same thing happened. Mom was frustrated that I couldn't eat. I couldn't even eat rice porridge.

The next day, I didn't get out of bed and stayed on the BiPAP because of the fear of running out of air. For the bathroom, I took the BiPAP with me. I was dependent on it. I didn't know why, though. I thought it was just a cold. I drank Ensure for nutrients. It was all I could do. I stayed in bed and on the BiPAP for a few days. I had the nasal mask on for so long my skin was wearing off. It stung and was irritated.

Mom came in and said, "Let's go to the doctor." "I don't want to," I said, shaking my head. "Why not?" she said with frustration. I didn't want to go because I had a pulmonary appointment the next day. She was worried. That night when my mom turned me, a few minutes later, I couldn't catch my breath. I was coughing too much. I called my mom again. She came in and said, "What now?" "Mom, I can't breathe," I said while trying to breathe. Mom and I were scared. "Turn me back on my back," I said. She did and I could breathe easier. But I was uncomfortable on my back. I kept calling Mom in.

She was frustrated and tired. She grabbed a chair and said, "I'll just sit here all night, then." She didn't, though.

The next day, I asked my mom to pack my BiPAP to take to my appointment. I was wearing my nasal mask. My brother, Jason, went also because we had the same appointment. We were meeting David Erickson there.

On the road, I thought my breathing wasn't good because I was dependent on the BiPAP. I had known for a while that my respiratory numbers were decreasing and were very low, close to zero. I was hoping that I would be approved for and be trying to use a non-invasive ventilator before this day would come—respiratory failure.

A non-invasive ventilator idea is using a ventilator without getting a tracheotomy, with no cutting or surgery. The ventilator hooks on the back of my power wheelchair with a straw-like tube placed next to my mouth. After a few shallow breaths, I just reach over and get a deep breath from the ventilator, which is on all the time.

As we got to the waiting room, David wasn't there yet. We went in. He saw us through the glass, seeing me with my mask on. I was looking frail and spent, like a gambler who had just put his last dollar on the table. While waiting, I suspected what was about to happen to me . . . something that I'd thought about, but only once in a while, for so long. "It" was something that I couldn't put out of my mind, since I could not figure out how having "it" would fit into my current home life.

I had this look on my face that matched my thoughts of "just shoot me." I said that at many stages of this little adventure of my life—it's a joke, but behind it was some truth. Sometimes, it seems that taking control of our lives by ending them is better than letting things just continue to go downhill and out of control.

David walked through the door and said something funny and sarcastic like he always does. "Hey Pedro, going scuba diving?" he said jokingly. "You funny, Dave," I said. I barely smiled. My life batteries were just about out of juice.

As we sat there in the waiting room, we could see other patients looking our way; some on oxygen, some just overweight and in poor health. I could see what they were thinking, "Wow, I don't feel so bad now, look at that skinny guy. He can't even catch his breath on a BiPAP . . ."

We talked of useless things until we entered the patient room for Dr. Gil. We saw Dr. Lake first; he was cool . . . almost sounded like he'd try and run with the whole non-invasive vent idea. It was about then that David stepped out of the room; he had to leave, unfortunately. But before he left, he saw Dr. Gil speaking to Dr. Lake. David realized that Dr. Gil would never go for the non-invasive vent, and that my health had deteriorated too far anyway. He told David it was "silly" to try the non-invasive vent. That was his word: "Silly."

Dr. Gil came in to do his checkup like always. He listened to my lungs with a stethoscope. "You have a collapsed left lung and you have pneumonia. We are going to admit you to the hospital tonight," he said with no surprise. "That bad, huh," I said jokingly. But it wasn't a joke though. The nurses called to get everything ready for me. As we waited, my brother called David and left a message. "My brother is in the hospital," he said. David already figured out that much. He wasn't surprised.

As we were waiting for the ambulance, I was thinking, "How long will I have to stay in the hospital? What's going to happen to me? What are the doctors going to suggest? And what will Mom do?" I was thinking about a lot of things. Mom was sleeping and my brother was trying to sleep. We were waiting for a few hours. The ambulance came after 5:30 p.m., after the doctor's office closed. In the ambulance, I used my own BiPAP. I can't use their ventilator because I don't have a trach. My mom and Jason followed us in the van.

I was admitted to the ER. My mom came with me while Jason stayed in the van. I thought that the nurse arranged a room at the ICU already. While waiting on the stretcher in the hallway, my BiPAP stopped working. "It's not working" I said in a scared voice. "What's not working?" mom said as she looked around. I was pointing at my BiPAP. She went to get a nurse. The nurse came and said, "We don't have anything like that." I panicked. My breathing became faster and harder. I was panting. My mom fiddled with the battery connection, and it started working again. I was relieved.

I finally got a bed around 8:30 p.m. I had to switch to their BiPAP. It was bigger than mine. I was uncomfortable on their bed. The mattress was hard and besides, I was too skinny. I had my mom reposition me often. It was crowed and noisy. There weren't enough beds. The nurses and doctors were running around like chickens without their heads on. It was hectic. It was getting late and mom was still with me. It was

9:30 p.m. Jason was still in the van waiting and hungry. We hadn't had dinner yet. I too was hungry. I wasn't worried about being hungry right then. My mind was busy. "Mom, take Jason home. I'll be fine." I said. Mom said, "Okay." She gave me a kiss on my forehead. "I'll be back," she said, walking off.

I had tests and x-rays done. It was freezing in there. Hospitals keep the temperature cold to keep the germs down. I had to wait on my nurse to get repositioned or for the urinal. My butt was hurting most of the time. I couldn't sleep—too much noise. I just watched all the commotion.

11:30 p.m. rolled around, and Mom and Dad came in. I didn't know Mom would be back that soon. Dad didn't talk much. He was concerned. "How are you?" he asked. "I'm fine . . . no big deal." I said with a slight smile. But I wasn't. They stayed for about forty minutes. I asked Mom to go home. It was late. "I can't just leave you," she said with tears running down her cheeks. "Mom, go home. I'll be fine. Please go." I said with a smile. So they left. I had to be strong for her.

Around 3:30 a.m. I was transferred to the ICU—finally. One of the nurses asked, "Can you go off the BiPAP?" I was scared and shook my head. "Just for few minutes," she said with a smile. I shook my head. So the nurse walked off to get their BiPAP. I was just waiting. I thought to myself, "Finally, a room is available." I didn't know what was going to happen to me in the ICU. The nurse came back wheeling a BiPAP. It was white with flashing lights. It was huge, bigger than mine. It had wheels. My BiPAP was in a carry bag. No hassle. The Respiratory Therapist (RT) switched me over to their portable machine. It felt weird. It took some time to get adjusted to the right settings. I was wheeled to the ICU along with a nurse pushing the BiPAP along side of me. We took the elevator to the seventh floor to the ICU, 7200. It was small. All the rooms were facing each other in a circle. In the middle, there was the nurse's station. Each room had two patients with one nurse. I got the bed next to the door.

I was transferred on the bed. Suddenly, I felt a pinch. "What was that?" I wondered. It was an IV line. The nurse started hooking me up to monitors for my vitals. The nurses were telling me things but I wasn't paying attention. I was very sleepy. I was getting poked with needles. They were drawing blood for tests. "More?" I asked. I just got blood drawn in the ER. But they needed to test my oxygen level in my blood every few hours. Blood was drawn from my wrist. It's painful and can numb my hand if they start "digging" for a vein.

When I tried to push the call light, I couldn't because I didn't have the strength to push it. I was concerned. "Do you have a sensitive button for me to use?" I said. "Yes, we do. But we can't get you one until later," the nurse said. My eyes opened wide. I need that call light because I can't call out for help if I need to. My nurse decided to stay in the room instead of sitting outside. I was relieved a bit. "Phew," I said.

That night I couldn't sleep. It was too cold and too much noise. I even took sleeping medication, but I was awake the whole night. I was in an unfamiliar place. The nurses were running all over the ward. It's hard not to notice through the window of the door. I was wondering what my family was going through, especially my mom.

Morning came; a radiologist came in with a portable x-ray machine. It was a box with a metal arm attached to the base. The radiologist can roll the x-ray under my bed while the arm hovers over me. He had to place the x-ray board behind my back. That was cold. It took five seconds to take. And he was out. "That's it," I said. I shrugged my shoulder. "What's going to happen next?" I said. I just closed my eyes and waited.

My nurse came in and introduced me to another nurse who was relieving her. The nurses switched every twelve hours. I didn't get the same nurse each day. Most of them were nice.

I got washed up by a CNA (Certified Nurse Assistant). Her name was Melissa Griffies. She brought in my breakfast. I was wearing my nasal mask and I couldn't eat. The RT came in to take off my mask so I could eat since Melissa wasn't allowed to. I could last for ten minutes off the BiPAP. The food was nasty. "Eww," I said. I couldn't eat that much. It was tiresome. I had to wait for the RT to put my nasal mask back on.

Hazel Rodriguez, my nurse, gave me my medicines. "One more," she said. I saw a syringe in her hand. "What's that?" I said. "It's a heparin shot. I'm going to inject this in your stomach," she said. "What's a heparin shot?" I asked. She said, "A heparin shot acts as an anticoagulant, preventing the formation of clots and extension of existing clots within the blood." It was painful since I was too skinny to have any cushion for the injection. I weighed sixty-nine pounds. "Why?" I said. "Because you're in bed too long," she said. I got that shot three times a day. My stomach was sore with red spots all over. I don't know why I need it since I laid in bed for long periods at home. I didn't get any blood clots.

I was friendly to everyone that came in my room: nurses, therapists, and CNAs. I remembered all their names. When I need help, whoever walks by my room I can call out. They usually stop and help me out.

I was not able to sleep for a few days. My eyes were red. I couldn't even doze off. I started to hallucinate a complete movie on the ceiling from start to finish. It was all red. It lasted for a few minutes. I blinked. "What was that just now," I wondered. I don't remember what the movie was about, but I do remember a red bicycle. It was weird.

Hazel brought in an easier call light that I could use. It was so sensitive to push. "Wow," I said. I was so relieved that I could use it. I wasn't scared anymore with the door closed. I was anxious when the nurse went out the room. I couldn't call out. Not enough air to do it. Having a call bell makes a big difference on the mind. The call bell was so sensitive that I accidentally rang it constantly. When I dozed off, my head would fall and hit the bell. It drove the nurses crazy.

I was hooked up to an I.V. line for hydration and nutrients, but it made me use the urinal constantly because the liquid is going directly in the blood stream and into the kidneys quickly. I was constantly ringing the bell. It was stressful because I had to go badly and I had to wait for my nurse or the CNA. Sometimes, I had to wait a long time. I almost had a few accidents because of that. The nurse asked me if I would want to use a condom catheter.

"A condom catheter is a rubber sheath that is put over your penis. A condom catheter allows you to empty your bladder without using a urinal, bedpan, or toilet.

It is hooked to a plastic tube which leads to a
bag." (Silvestri)

I hated it because if the condom catheter gets twisted or
kinked the urine flows back and leaks all over. It was a hassle
because the CNA has to change the sheets while I'm in bed.
After each time I urinate, I asked my nurse or the CNA to
check if the condom catheter was kinked or twisted or not.
"Better safe than sorry," I said.

I hated the bed baths they gave me. I got one every night. It
was freezing. I was shivering the whole time even though the
water was warm. My mom would help when she was visiting.
Two got it done quicker. The hard part about the bed bath was
being careful not to disconnect all the wires I was connected
to, or break the IV line in my arm. It took a while to warm up.
I had to use three blankets.

I was so skinny, my butt—the ischial tuberosity (IT)—was
always uncomfortable lying in bed. I was calling to be
repositioned all the time. The nurses were frustrated with me.
I told David about it. He brought in cushions for me to try, but
I was still uncomfortable. "Ouch," I said as my mom came in
and said, "What's wrong?" David explained to her and she
calmed down. I'm glad she was there. She would reposition
me when I needed. David came back with a smile. "What are
you smiling about?" I said. "I have these," he said holding out
a small bag. He took out two round gel pads. "Breasts," he
said. "What? I don't need breast implants." I smiled. We all
laughed. He placed them under each of my ITs while my mom
helped. It felt weird, soft and squishy. It was so comfortable.
The drawback of them was when I turn on my side or on my

back, the gel pads need to be positioned right each time. They were a hassle, but they worked.

Ashly came to visit. She was feeding me chicken noodle soup and I started having a hard time catching my breath. I called the nurse to get the RT. She came in. "What's wrong?" she asked. "Hard to breathe," I said. She got me breathing treatments:

> "Albuterol nasal inhalant and chest percussions. Albuterol is a bronchodilator that relaxes muscles in the airways and increases air flow to the lungs. Chest percussion involves striking the palm side of a cupped hand along the center of the upper rib cage downward until the bottom of the rib cage. The cupping will deliver a maximal vibration that will penetrate the chest cavity, bronchial tree, and into the depths of the lungs loosen thick mucous secretions. Once loosened, the action of the cilia (tiny hairs that direct the flow of air and sputum) will clear the mucus and restore your fuller breathing capacity." (Silvestri)

The treatments didn't work. Ashly was holding my hands. I was still gasping for air. She started crying. Then David walked through the door. "What's happened?" he asked. I shook my head. "Not good," I said softly. I started panicking. That made it worse on everyone. The RT was trying everything. Nothing worked. She was puzzled. And she's an RT? She had my life in her hands. Scary. My nurse was in tears. I looked at David and said, "Use the full facial mask." He rushed over and got the Ambu bag with the full facial mask connected to it. It covers my mouth and nose. He started pushing air into me. I felt relieved. Then I started coughing and I cleared something from my throat. I spit it out and it was dark brown. "It was a mucous plug," I said. That long to figure that out? A mucus plug is dried mucous lodged in my throat blocking the airway which I was unable to clear. "I got air finally," I said. "Good job of thinking to get the Ambu bag," David said. I smiled. I almost died. I'm glad that my mom wasn't there to see what I had to go through. It would be very hard on her. Ashly was torn up emotionally.

Dr. Gil and Dr. Lake came in to see how I was doing. "How are you feeling today?" asked Dr. Gil. "I feel better," I said. "That's good to hear," said Dr. Lake. I smiled. I kind of knew why they were here. I was telling myself that I had to make a decision on getting a tracheotomy or not. They both asked me. I didn't answer. "You'll feel better, breathe easier, eat better, and have a better quality of life," Dr. Gil said with a smile. "I'm still hopeful that I can get better and be able to use the non-invasive ventilator. I am getting better," I said. "It's best for you to get a tracheotomy, but let us know what you decide, okay," he said. I nodded. Then they left.

The next day, the RT came in with an oxygen tank-like thing, with a straw like tube connected on the side. It was their version of a non-invasive ventilator. I tried it but I couldn't reach it to get a breath of air. The RT had to come in to give me a breath. That sucks. That's not what I wanted. I wanted to be able to take a breath on my own.

The Physical Therapist (PT) came in every morning to do range of motion so I won't lose my range of my limbs. If I don't get range of motion, my ligaments get stiff and tight. My range would be very limited. "Once I lose it, it's gone forever," I said. "You're absolutely right," he smiled. I had my power wheelchair in the room that mom brought earlier. The PT wanted me to sit up in my wheelchair. "Okay," I said. The nurses, the RT, and David were there, ready to put me in my wheelchair. They were careful because of all the wires that were connected to me. I was told that I might feel dizzy sitting up after being in bed for a long time. When I was in my wheelchair finally, the nurses asked, "How are you feeling?" "Fine. I don't feel any difference," I said. I smiled at everyone. The charge nurse was watching my stats on the monitor. A few minutes later, my heart rate was 130 beats per minute (BPM) and still rising. He was concerned. "Are you sure you're okay? Your heart rate is high," he said. "Yeah," I nodded. My heart rate jumped up to 180 BPM. That is way too high. The strange part was that I didn't feel my heart beat fast. The charge nurse said, "He should get back in bed right now!" My heart could have jumped out of my chest at any time.

David mentioned a group home called Angel View that I could go to if I got trached and ventilated. David Erickson is an Occupational Therapist Consultant for Angel View also. He told me that it's in the desert. It's a four room house with six residents. There are two nurses and two direct care staff on each shift, eight hour shifts. It's more of a home-like environment. "If I set it up, will you go?" he asked. "I don't know," I said.

Dr. Gil came in and said, "It's been a week. Have you decided what you want to do?" I shook my head. "We need to know. You can't stay here forever," said Dr. Gil. "I know," I said while looking away. "You're smart enough to know what comes next. You did the research on MD at home," he said calmly. I nodded. He left the room. "In a body bag or go home with a morphine drip bag to die," I said softly.

The next night, Mom came to visit like she always does. I told her what the doctors had asked me. After a few minutes, she said, "What are you going to do? Get the machine and go home? I don't know how to take care of you with the machine." She started crying. She sat down and took out a pack of tissues. I couldn't bear to see my mom like that. I turned my head away. Tears were coming down my cheeks. "What should I do?" I said. I thought to myself, "Why do I want to get ventilated and keep going with life when Mom is like this? Maybe I should just leave this world. Ahh!" I shook my head with sadness. Then my mom said, "I don't want you to die." She was holding my hand with tears coming down her cheeks. It was difficult for me to see my mom cry. I said, "Okay, Mom, I'll get the tracheotomy and ventilator and we'll find a way to fit this in our lives." Mom nodded.

I thought about the facility David mentioned before. "Maybe I should go there," I said out loud. "You going to do that?" she replied. I nodded. Mom's facial expression lit up a little. I also thought about my younger brother Jason. Maybe I can show him what kind of a life I can have, living with a ventilator. Then he can honestly decide what to do when his time comes. David came in after an hour and I asked him, "Can you still get me in to Angel View?" "Why?" he asked. I told him that I'm ready to make a decision now. "About what?" he said. But he knew. "I'm ready to take the dive now," I smiled. "Are you sure?" he smiled. "Yeah," I nodded. "I'll start making the arrangements for you," he said happily. David took out his cell phone and started dialing. "You won't regret it," he said. And he stepped out of the room to talk to Angel View's head of the QIDPs (Qualified Intellectual Disabilities Professional).

David had said this about me: "You had years to think about this but, when it came down to it, worrying about what your mom would do with you vented was at the top of your mind, I think. NOT your personal well-being, but hers. Very noble as a son. I know that for several days, as you struggled so hard against the pneumonia, so hard against trying to eat, so hard against life . . . taking care of your mom was what you thought about most."

David said, "I think only when living at Angel View became a possibility did you look to that option. Without a place to go, without a plan to keep your mom from being your caretaker, I think you would have just left us."

Afterward, he briefly told me about the other five residents living there already. I saw a bit of relief from mom. Mom said, "It's getting late. We had better go." "Yeah," I said. As I lay there, I wondered if it will be okay. I went to sleep.

**Tubes**

The next day, Dr. Lake came in to check up on me. "Peter, have you made a decision yet?" he asked. "I'm going to get the tracheotomy," I said. "Good. You'll breathe easier. You'll be able to eat better. No more mask," he explained. "Can I get a G-Tube inserted as well?" I asked. "Of course. I'll get it all set up," he smiled.

David had said to me:

"When you made the decision to be trached and to move to Angel View, I saw a small flicker of light begin to shine in your eyes again. It wasn't bright, but it was there: you had a plan. Amazing things are possible when humans have a plan . . . when you can see beyond the torture of right now, and see into the future . . . to your plan. With your plan in mind, you began to heal. First the trach, then the G-Tube, then all those weeks of antibiotics . . . you were often weak and tired, often defeated, but you never gave up. You picked it back up and kept going."

15 December 2006, my family and David came to see me off before the surgery. Mom gave me a kiss on my forehead. Then they went to the waiting room to wait. The nurses got me ready for the surgery. They rolled me to surgery with my bed. It was freezing in there. "Ready?" the surgeon asked. I nodded. He placed an oxygen mask over my mouth and nose and turned on the anesthesia. I was knocked out.

**Dave's Part/Trach**

[15 December 2006. "I awoke with a start. Today my friend and patient Peter would get his tracheotomy surgery, forever creating a pathway for the air he so desperately has been without. The surgery is called a tracheotomy; it creates a hole just below the Adam's apple which allows air to enter the trachea directly. The surgery goes fast, usually less than 30 minutes. I arrived at the hospital to find his family sitting around waiting. They all spoke of the coming surgery. Some with fear, others not really sure what to expect. Peter was reasonably comfortable on the full mask BiPAP. He has been on the NG tube for feedings so the mask could stay on. In the later afternoon, they begin to prep Peter for his surgery. We all wished him well, I joked about how he won't remember a thing. He says "Yes I will," more mouthing those words than speaking them. I've already warned him that he will not be able to speak after the surgery. The trach installed during surgery will have a balloon around it to keep all the air coming into his trachea going to his lungs, so none of it can come upwards over his vocal cords and escape out his nose/ mouth. They will keep this balloon inflated for a week or so. We'll resort to mouthing words (there will be no more mask in the way) or finger spelling. His family is anxious as orderlies take Peter away. I suggest that we all walk down to the Children's Hospital cafeteria and sit, I can better explain what is happening and what to expect after this surgery and into the future.

Everyone seems relieved to have something to do. We wander down the hall to the elevator, down to the first floor cafeteria. The kitchen is closed, but the vending machines are open and we get drinks and sit. I explain the surgery, the white plastic trach that they will see in his throat. How he won't be able to speak for a few weeks, but will eventually figure out how to speak over the trach and will even learn to sprint (breathing off the ventilator) for up to a few hours. Right now, all we wish for Peter is that he gets some air. None of us is really sure how he has made it this long.

I remind them that the gag reflex is located nearby where the trach will stick into his trachea, causing him to make gagging sounds and faces for the next day or so. It can look quite disturbing, I tell them, but really isn't as uncomfortable as it looks. After 20 minutes or so, we rise and wander back to the elevators, back up to his floor. Everyone is in a group close together. I am sort of leading the way, we pass in front of Peter's room, where his bed should be empty as he just left 25 minutes ago for surgery. He is there! Just as everyone looks in to see him, he gags, makes a horrible face and blood runs down his neckline into his gown. Argh! I hear Peter's aunt say she is going to be sick. Everyone has a look of horror on his or her face. What have I done? I had planned on taking them back to the waiting room, making sure he was cleaned up nicely and then bringing a few of them in to see him at a time. That surgery was less than 15 minutes. After apologizing to the family and leaving them off at the waiting room answering a few questions along the way, I returned to his room.

He was alert and said he remembers everything. We joked about a certain person's shirt color, and he remembered it correctly. Now, just minutes since his trach surgery, he is alert and we are "talking." He is resting now, no more mask on his face. At 16:45 today, he started his new life. A mechanically dependent one, but a new one at that. His next battle is to get over his pneumonia.

Later, maybe an hour after, he has come out of the rest of the sedation, and was cleaned up. I brought a few family members in to see him, especially since they saw him so quickly after the surgery. His Aunt didn't think she could do it, but I assured her that he was fine and looked fine; she entered the room with trepidation, but Peter threw her a smile and all was well. His mom was scared but happy that at last her boy could breathe. Various other family; brothers, sister, cousins, uncles and his dad, all come through at one point or another. His family finally goes home, but I stayed until 21:00. It was a long day for everyone. Now that he was trached, the pressure was on to find him a place to live, as returning home in this newly medically-fragile condition would not fit into the family model that his family lived in. First thing tomorrow morning, I'll be on the phone trying to find a place for Peter to call home."]

I woke up and felt something lodged into my neck. My throat was sore. I couldn't talk. I looked across my bed and saw tubes coming from my neck. My eyes were wide open. "How are you feeling?" the nurse asked. "A little sore," I said but no sound is coming out. I was puzzled. I looked at my nurse and she said, "Silly me; I forgot you won't be able to talk for a while," pointing at the bottom of her neck. "Oh," I said quietly. "Don't worry, you'll be able to talk again," she smiled. Then she left. The RT came in and explained to me why I couldn't talk. He said, "Well, there's a cuff balloon around the tracheotomy inside, so there won't be any air leakage. The air blows out the exhalation valve before the air passages through your diaphragm. No air reaching there, no sound. There is one way to talk for now. I would have to deflate the balloon but you're newly trached." I nodded. For the first time, in a long time, I can actually get a satisfying breath with no difficulty and without having to catch the next breath. I felt so relieved not having the feeling of suffocation anymore. I was able to eat a full meal without gasping for air. I enjoyed it.

My family came in. Mom was almost in tears. I wonder why. They asked me questions but all they see was my mouth moving. Melissa came in and said, "Wow, I can see your face and I could understand you now." I smiled at her.

A few days of getting used to a trach, it wasn't what I expected. It was a weird feeling using the ventilator. I still tried breathing naturally and the ventilator gave me a breath. I was getting extra breaths. I had to let the ventilator breathe for me. It was something I had to get used to fast. I couldn't communicate and it was very difficult and frustrating for everyone. Talking was all I had left. I couldn't tell anyone what I needed help with. The nurses would get frustrated and impatient with me. David and I wrote out a cheat sheet of certain things I would need assistance with: need to turn, have to use the urinal, etc. That helped a little but I couldn't explain the little details on how I want assistance. I could wait for the RT to deflate the balloon but that'll take a while to get done. There was only one RT on duty. The RT did have time. It's not like there are many patients with respiratory problems. The only way I could actually communicate was using my eyes. I would just look at my limbs and I would wiggle my hand or foot and then the nurse would then ask some questions regarding what assistance are needed. It also works for the toileting or for the urinal. It was easy to do that.

20 December 2006, the nurse was explaining to me about the G-Tube procedure which would be done in my room. The technicians came in with the portable x-ray machine and all the equipment necessary for the surgery. The nurse inserted the I.V. line on my hand for a drug called Vercid (Midazolam). It's used to produce sleepiness or drowsiness and to relieve anxiety before surgery. It is also used to produce loss of consciousness before and during surgery. The gastroenterologist told me that I won't remember the surgery afterward. I said, "Okay." I was injected with the Vercid and I nodded off and woke up instantly. I thought that I would be asleep. The gastroenterologist took out a black tube-like scope. She was applying a numbing agent on the scope. "What's that for?" I asked. She said, "I'm going to put this down your throat to see where I'm going to put the G-Tube." She put the scope down my throat and I didn't feel it go down nor did I gag. She turned the monitor on so I can see the scope going

down my esophagus. "Ooh," I said. It was a pink wall with green vines (veins) all over. She stopped a little bit in the stomach. "You're going to feel a pinch around your stomach," she said with a smile. She took out a long needle with a numbing agent and injected me. My stomach went numb. On the monitor, I saw a hook being hooked on the wall of my stomach. Then a small tube showed on the monitor. The doctor tied the tube to the hook. "That's the G-Tube," she said. It didn't even hurt. "All done," she said. "That's it," I said. "Yup," she said with a smile. Then she left. The other doctor asked a question about the date. I answered him. "Why is he fully aware?" he asked the nurses. They shrugged their shoulders. The nurses didn't inject me with enough Vercid. I remember the whole procedure. I wasn't supposed to. My family and David came in to see how I was doing. I told them what happened.

It felt weird having a tube sticking out of my stomach. The G-Tube felt like it was turning inside my stomach. It was turning because the stomach is trying to close the incision. I also had muscle cramping around the G-Tube area. It hurt too. I had an x-ray done later that night to check up on the G-Tube. It was fine. The drawback of having a G-Tube is that when getting repositioned in bed, it can be tugged or even get pulled out. I had to be cautious about it. The good things are I don't have to eat when I don't feel like it. I can just get a can of nutrients down my G-Tube. If I don't want to taste nasty medicine, I just take that through the G-Tube.

# 9. In Transition

## Subacute

After a few days of observation, the doctors wanted to discharge me. David was asking the discharge planner to let me stay for another week, but to no avail. "Money reasons," the discharge planner had said. David was telling me that a bed hasn't opened up yet at Angel View So he was going to have to find me a place to park for a week. He knew a place for me close by the hospital. "What kind of place and how bad is it?" I asked. He said, "A community hospital; in the adult subacute ward."

A subacute hospital is basically a permanent intensive care unit (ICU), having the monitors and respiratory staff to support patients living on ventilators and other mechanical means (G-Tubes, dialysis etc). Subacute patients are usually stable but unable to reduce their dependence on ventilators or other mechanical supports. The subacute gives those patients an existence in a supported environment.

Staffing is not what one would hope for in a subacute. Most patients are comatose to some degree or another, staff is often busy with other patients. Being alert and oriented and living in a subacute unit is very challenging. Everything that happens in the subacute is related to maintenance. Most patients have been through rehab and other inpatient therapies, having made poor gains there, so that very little active treatment to move someone forward occurs here in the subacute. Staff are often not appreciative of a patient's ability to "ring the call bell" for help.

All in all, the subacute environment is not a good one, seen as a place for patients to be "parked" until they die is often an accurate description. A nursing home or Skilled Nursing Facility is usually considered a step down from a subacute, that is, a lesser level of care, although many SNF's have units for ventilators and other similar type patients from those found in subacutes.

"If you can avoid a SNF or subacute, do it! It's bad but better than all the other ones." I looked at him and shook my head. David said, "Sorry. It's the best I can do." "Fine. It's only for a week," I said. David nodded and he left the room to get that started with the discharge planner. I said to myself, "This is going to be bad," while shaking my head.

The next day it was done. That was fast because there was an opening. "When am I leaving?" I said out loud. The discharge planner said, "In two days. The 24th." I looked at them both with uncertainty. I really didn't want to go, but I had no choice. I couldn't go home to wait for Angel View. It would've been great if it did happen. "Only a week, right?" I asked firmly. David nodded. "Oh well, it's only a week. I can handle another week," I said. I told myself, "It's time to be a tough sissy."

24 December 2006, the nurses and the staff were telling me how much of an inspiration I was to them. I never thought about being an inspiration to anyone. I was just being myself and trying to live. Melissa said, "You are an inspiration to me and others. You're a strong person and always have a smile on your face. I'm glad I met you." I thanked her for taking good care of me. She smiled. Everyone took good care of me there. I didn't want to leave. I told her I don't want to go to a subacute. "It'll be okay. You're a strong person. You can handle anything. Besides, it's only a week, right?" she said. I nodded and thanked her. She also added, "And Peter, don't lose that smile." She gave me a hug and left.

Later that night, it was time for me to get discharged. My mom, Anh and Jimmy came in to see me off. The Emergency Medical Technician (EMT) came in with a stretcher and brought their ventilator. I was thinking to myself, "It's all the same." I didn't know that much about ventilators. I was transferred onto the stretcher and still connected to the hospital ventilator. The RT switched me over. It felt wrong. I wasn't getting the right amount of air and the wrong breath rate. I kind of panicked. I was immediately bagged and switched back to the hospital ventilator. That scared me for a bit. My mom was scared and almost in tears. "Mom, I'm okay. Don't worry." I said calmly.

The EMT was trying to figure out what was wrong with their ventilator. Apparently, both ventilators were different. The EMT was using a pressure ventilator. A pressure ventilator is a ventilator that allows the user to initiate a breath of how much volume of air the user wants. The user can initiate a shallow or a deep breath. I was using a volume ventilator. A volume ventilator lets the user initiate a breath but will receive their volume of air that was preset by their doctor.

That was my problem with the EMT's ventilator. I wouldn't have been able to initiate a deep enough breath. I felt short of breath on a pressure ventilator. But I was told the EMT didn't have a volume ventilator, and the hospital didn't allow me to borrow theirs for the ride. I really didn't have a choice. I said to myself, "Just suck it up," and I got on the pressure ventilator. I was on my way. My family and David went ahead to the subacute to meet me there. All I had on was a gown and a few blankets. Mom said it was very cold out there. I nodded without realizing what I had on. As soon as I got out to the parking lot, a gust of wind blew past me. I was freezing my butt off. The EMT quickly put me in the ambulance. I got my vitals done. They were getting my paperwork done. I was trying not to panic for air. One of the EMT guys was talking to me to keep me calm. The drive was only twenty minutes.

As we pulled up to the subacute, they took me out. It was so cold. David was waiting for us at the entrance. "What took you guys so long?" he asked. I said, "Traffic." So I was wheeled in the building into a white hallway. Lights shining brightly and the staff watching as I went by. As I got in my room, I saw my roommate unresponsive. The room smelled like urine. It was tiny, maybe 8' by 16'. The room was dull, just white walls and a window with a view of a building and a tree. The atmosphere in there was depressing and gloomy. The RT was there as I was being transferred over to the bed while being careful of the tubes. I was being bagged with an Ambu bag. Switching over to the other ventilator had the same weird feeling I had with the EMT's. It took me twenty minutes to get used to. I asked the staff how the care was. "Good," they said.

"What's the patient-to-nurse ratio?" I asked. The nurse said, "Twelve patients to one nurse." I looked at David and family with a grin. "This is going to get bad," I blurted out.

The mattress was too hard to lie on. I needed more pillows, so we asked the CNA for one. Her response was, "We're sorry, we're only allowed to give you two." My mom's mouth dropped. Good thing I had a pillow from the ICU.

The staff wasn't prepared to take me. I tried the call light that was connected to the bed. I couldn't push it. I looked at David and he knew that a call bell was essential to my care. He asked the nurse if they have a call light that I could push. The staff said, "Not really." David was arguing for one for ten minutes. I believe they gave me a hard time for a call light because they didn't want to be bothered with me since most of their patients were comatose. They can't call. Nice and quiet shifts. They were worried that I would call constantly and be needy.

Then the nurse finally said that I can get one by tonight. I was relieved to hear that. I wanted to get to know all the staff's names and let them know about my condition and that I could feel everything. The CNA and the nurse were telling me my schedule. Rise and shine at 6 a.m. Breakfast is at 6:30 a.m. Lunch will be at noon. Dinner will be around six. Shower will be twice a week on Tuesdays and Fridays in the evening. I asked the CNA, "How will I take a shower with the ventilator?" "We'll roll you in the shower with a shower gurney and we'll bag you with an Ambu bag," she said. I wasn't too sure about showering like that. "We have activities once a day in the activities' room," she said with a smile. She told me that it's to watch movies and stuff. I was thinking,

"With whom?" The RT left after I was situated on the ventilator.

It was freezing in there. I had two blankets on and was still freezing. I asked for another blanket which helped a bit. But I was still cold. I asked to be turned on my side. Their response was, "The law says we are only allowed to reposition you every two hours." David and I were stunned. My mom was shocked. And they said, "We give good care."

The nurse came back in with a bottle of something. She said, "It's your feeding." I looked at her with a confused look on my face. "What feeding?" I said. "Well, you have to eat, you know," she said with a smile. I explained to her that I was eating by mouth at the ICU. I had a swallow evaluation and passed. She didn't buy it. She told me that I had a G-Tube which made me NPO (nothing by mouth). David said, "What!" I was thinking the same thing. I was too tired to fight it. She hooked me up to the feeding and left. "What the hell was that?" I asked David and my family. My family didn't know. David suggested that the nurse didn't want to take the time to feed me. We all believed that.

It was getting late, so my mom and David were getting me comfortable in bed. They repositioned my "breast implants" under my IT's; they fixed the pillows and blankets just right. Mom gave me the urinal. Anh and Jimmy had just left. The nurse brought in a call light for me. It was a big medium yellow button which had a long cord that can be connected to the call light system. I was barely able to push it. That would have to do. Mom was worried about the bell. I asked my mom to go home and get some rest and to take care of Jason. He was at home waiting. Mom gave me a kiss on my forehead and said, "I love you." Before she left, I said it back to her. Then David left.

As I was lying in bed thinking, it was weird that mom would give me a kiss and say, "I love you." We never say stuff like that. I guessed after something like not being able to breathe and the possibility of death would bring my family closer than we had ever been. It would take me to get trached for this to happen. That was a good thing.

I tried to get some sleep that night but couldn't. I was in pain from my skinny butt, too bony, on the hard mattress. The pain felt like my skin was going to get ripped apart from my butt. I tried to ring my call light but couldn't; it slipped out of my hand when I dozed off. I was "finger walking" to try to feel for the call light but couldn't find it. I panicked and called out for help a few times, but the CNA didn't come. The pain was great, and I was trying to keep my mind off the pain. I began to get anxious and started trying to get off the pressure to relieve the pain. All it takes is to be repositioned just a tiny bit.

It was a workout, and I was sweating. I got frustrated and moved my hand, and I felt the call light. A sigh of relief, I grabbed it and kept pushing it, but no one came in until thirty minutes later. I was getting lectured from the CNA about "It's not two hours yet" speech. "What great care, they say," I said as I rolled my eyes at him. He repositioned me after all that. "I won't be back till two hours later, okay?" he said. I said, "Whatever." I shut my eyes and shook my head with frustration knowing that I will have to get repositioned again before the two hours is up. It was getting late, so I stopped thinking about it and tried to fall asleep. In about ten minutes I was asleep.

A new CNA came in and woke me up at 7 a.m. It was the staff's shift change. She took my vitals and said, "I'll be back to clean you up," and left. I went back to sleep.

The CNA came in at 8 a.m. and woke me up. She opened the curtains and said, "Rise and shine." I replied, "Yeah, I can rise from the bed." She laughed and said, "You're funny." I wasn't being funny. I was in a bad mood and tired because of the sleepless night I had from all the pain. She gave me a bed bath and changed the sheets and my gown. I was wary of my tubes getting pulled. I was freezing and shivering. "I'll be done in a minute," she smiled. Next, she brushed my teeth and washed my face. "All cleaned," she said. Then she asked me which way I wanted to turn. I turned toward the window. As she turned me, she wasn't being careful of the tubes. The tube was tugged and I end up choking because the tube was pushing against my throat. That made me cough so hard I had tears coming down my cheek and my chest ached. My throat was irritated and I became congested. I hated getting suctioned. Since I can't cough out my secretion, the RT would push a suction catheter inside my tracheotomy and pull out slowly while suctioning the secretion out so I can breathe. The RT came in to do trach care.

The RT suggested that I tie the call bell to my wrist so I won't lose it again. He got one of the trach ties and wrapped the call bell wire to my wrist. It worked great. It was comfortable and it didn't get in the way at all.

As I stared out the window, it was Christmas and felt sad. This was the first Christmas that I'll be spending alone. I thought about my family, who's coming, who's not coming, the food they might serve, the gifts everyone will get, and the laughter and smiles. But instead I'm stuck here, miserable. I kept my mind off of what I'm missing at home. I knew my mom was coming later.

In the afternoon, a volunteer came in my room with a few things in his hand. He told me that he had a whole bag of stuff and was giving patients something for Christmas. When he got to my room, he had a stuffed animal and a handmade angel left. I took the angel. That was nice of him to do that. Not many patients have family to visit them.

That evening my mom, Anh and Jimmy came in. My sister brought me a small Christmas tree. She made it out of gold and red construction paper. It had gold lettering on each layer of the tree. Each layer had encouraging quotes written on it. And it had a small star on top.

After everyone left, I was finally going to get a shower—my first in three weeks. It was ten o'clock. I didn't know what to expect or how they're going to shower me or where the shower is for that matter. Two CNAs, two girls, came in. They explained to me how they were going to do the shower. I was asked if I could sit up in a shower chair. I shook my head. One CNA went out. "We have the water running, so it will get hot enough," one of them said. She got my gown off. The other CNA came back wheeling in a white plastic gurney. "What's that?" I asked. She said, "We're going to shower you while you're lying down." Then I thought that the ventilator was coming with me. I was okay with the shower since I have that. I was all pumped up and everything. The RT came in to help my tubes and the ventilator. They carefully slide me off the bed and onto the gurney. "No big deal," I said. It was cold. The RT got the blanket and covered me.

One of the CNAs took out an Ambu bag. "What's that for?" I asked with shock. "Well, one of us will be using the Ambu bag while the other will be showering you," she said. "What! I'm going to be bagged?" I was horrified. I was just trached and they expect me to be comfortable getting bagged. "Yeah, right." The shower doesn't sound so great. But I needed a shower badly. My hair was so flaky and itchy. I know I smell and my skin had soap residue from the bed baths. I just shrugged my shoulders and went along with it. The RT unhooked my tubes and inserted the Ambu bag on to my trach.

Then I was wheeled out the door and I was looking around to see where the shower was. It was just outside my door. The shower was a big empty yellow room only with the shower and curtain. The water was still cold. When they were washing my hair, water was sprayed on my face. I panic because for some reason I was afraid of water running down my face. Maybe, because of having a trach, I might be afraid the water would leak in my lungs through the trach. My breathing became erratic and needed bigger breaths, but they weren't paying attention to what they were doing. I was getting shallow breaths. I ended up panting for air. My heart rate jumped up from working too hard from breathing and shivering from the cold. Being anxious didn't help either.

When someone uses an Ambu bag on someone, he or she needs to pay attention. They were just showering away and talking to each other. "When are they going to be done?" I kept asking myself. When they said they were done, I was relieved. I was wheeled back to the room and couldn't wait to get on the ventilator. They transferred me back to my bed. The

RT switched me back on the ventilator. "Finally, enough air," I sighed. I'm never doing that again. But I was clean.

When I have to use the urinal or bed pan, I would have to wait an hour or two for an aide to come. By that time, I really had to go to the point of peeing or pooping on myself. That's how bad it was. The nurses don't usually give the urinals or bed pans but there are a few that would go out of their way to do them. Those are the ones that care regardless of their positions. There aren't many of those nurses out there. Since I was on tube feeding and on IV drip antibiotics, I had to urinate often. I constantly had to ring the bell to use the urinal or bed pan. The staff were annoyed with me for calling all the time. I did have a few accidents because of their neglect. Why don't they just give me the urinal or bed pan? I mean it's easier to clean a urinal or bed pan instead of cleaning up a big mess. When I had an accident, it meant that a CNA would have to change everything: bed sheets while I'm on there, my gown, and wiping. That made them even more frustrated at me. It's not my fault but theirs. The staff ended being so frustrated at me about the urinal; they ended up putting a condom catheter on me just to stop me from calling so much.

Then the head nurse decided that I was too anxious about having to use the urinal or repositioning. Basically, the staff are saying that I'm too needy and bothering their breaks. I was given a drug called Ativan to help me with my so called anxiety. I was given Ativan every six hours via G-Tube. I end up being an Ativan junkie. When it was almost time for the next dose, I always had my eyes on the clock. "*Fifteen more minutes . . . ten minutes more . . . five minutes more . . . yay, I can ring for more,*" I said like a crackhead. I did need Ativan because I was stuck in this bad place. I felt that my life had ended. I was in bed all day and hooked up to this tube all the time. I was depressed and wanted to give up. There was nothing to do except watch TV. But I knew I wouldn't be here much longer. Ativan was a way for me to be numb and not have to think about anything. It was a way to pass the time while staring at the wall.

I was still having a lot of secretion. I was still able to cough it out on my own. The nurses wanted me to spit it out, but where? At the top of my bed or anyone else's bed, there's a suction device on the wall with a long tubing connected to a Yankauer. I can't do it myself, so I would have to call a CNA to help me. But then, the staff began to get frustrated at me for calling too much. Later on, the RT came in to give me a suction and he had a great idea. He taped the Yankauer to my pillow next to my face, so I can get a suction whenever I wanted because it was on all the time. There were two bad things about that: it was making a suctioning noise constantly and when turning, the staff would have to tape the Yankauer to the pillow just right. It was a pain to do. I was spitting constantly. It was yucky. I filled up the canister the yankauer was connected to. The gunk was thick, brown and green. The Yankauer became my new best friend.

I got another swallow evaluation. The speech therapist did the test. I was given three substances to swallow while being x-rayed. Each substance had a different texture and thickness, from liquid to chunky. It was nasty because a blue dye was mixed in, so the x-ray can see the substance being swallowed. This test was to see if food will go down the right tube and not into my lungs. That can cause choking, aspiration, and even pneumonia. I passed with flying colors. I could eat now. And I get to taste again. I was so happy. I was craving for food but it's more about tasting. I was on tube feeding for a week. I was looking forward to fried chicken. When I got it, it tasted bad with no taste. What's the point? The Jell-O was great. But then eventually, the staff didn't have time to feed me. I was only given tube feeding. I was like, "Whatever."

David started telling me about the house that I was going to. I was going to a house called Jack Surnow House named after a donor. Angel View has nineteen homes. Then he mentioned Terri Thompson. She's the Q of Surnow. "What's a Q and what does one do?" I said. A Q is actually a QIDP (Qualified Intellectual Disability Professional) and is a client advocate, the legal person responsible for the operations of the house. "She's a great Q," David said.

The doctor, who comes in once a week, wanted to get a sputum culture from me to see if I still had pneumonia. My mom was in the room at the time when the nurse came in to get my sputum. I didn't cough it out on the petri dish. Since I had a trach, the nurse just performed a suction. That way the sample will come directly from the source. As the nurse was done, I guess she had to do a lab on my roommate. My mom watched her as she did the test. Later, my mom told me, "The nurse used your needle syringe with your test on your roommate at first." I didn't really pay attention, so I didn't think anything of it. The next day, the nurse came in and told me that I have the MRSA bug. Methicillin-resistant Staphylococcus Aureus is a bacterium that causes infections in different parts of the body. This infection is difficult to treat because it's a "resistance bug." MRSA is resistant to a group of antibiotics called the beta-lactams. It is spread by contact by touching another person who has it on their skin or touching objects that have the bacteria on them. I didn't know what it was. The doctor wanted me to take a strong IV antibiotic for it. I agreed to it. The next day the MRSA was gone. Must have been a mistake.

When David told me that Terri was coming for a visit with the director of nurses (D.O.N.) for Angel View, I didn't know what to expect. "They're just visiting to get an assessment of who you are and to see if you have any behavior problems, which you don't have. Don't worry about it. You'll probably be the best resident of the house," he said. I wasn't too worried then. I tried to look my best for them but I was ignored by staff. I wore my favorite gown just like everyone else. As they walked in the room, they were short, almost the same height, about 5'4." Terri had blonde hair and was wearing a black sweater. She sounded nice. She told me that they're here to make an assessment to see if AV can take care of me and know what supplies and equipment they would need. After the assessment, they felt that AV will be able to take care of me. I was so glad because all I wanted to do was to get out of this place. Anywhere but here. "Is there a time frame when AV will take me?" I asked. "Two weeks," she said. As she was about to leave, she said, "I hope you don't get pneumonia again."

I smiled. I had something to look forward to. There was a patient that David knew. He got her a power wheelchair. She was hit by a car. She's on a ventilator. I was told that she's been living in this subacute ward for twenty years. All she does is roll up and down the halls all day and sometimes visiting me. "What kind of life is that?" I asked myself. I don't want that kind of life. If I had known that, I wouldn't have gotten ventilated.

The subacute offered activities to their patients. I went to their activities room. I had to try and get out of bed. It's unhealthy to stay in bed all day and I was fully aware of what will happen if I do. I could lose my current physical abilities that I had left. The CNA came in with a chair that I was being transferred to, with wheels of course. The seat cushion was hard as a rock. It was uncomfortable. My legs were spread outward due to my contractures of the hip. The nurse got pillows to prop up my legs. As I was wheeled in the activities' room, there were other patients on ventilators already there watching a movie. As I observed them, there wasn't any movement and no signs of interest from them. A few of them were old, maybe in their sixties. It looks like they were there for a long time. It felt dead in the room. I don't know if they were brain dead or not. I watched the movie but my butt was getting sore from the seat. I couldn't wait till the movie ended.

Finally, the movie ended. The activities person wheeled me back to my room. She placed me next to my bed in front of the TV. Then she left. "That's it. Oh, well," I said. So I watched whatever was on. Thirty minutes later I had to use the urinal badly. I rang my call bell. Of course no one came in. I was holding it for a while. The charge nurse walked by my door, and I called her. She stopped and came in. I told her and she said, "In a moment." She left. I waited and waited. Fifteen minutes went by . . . twenty minutes . . . forty minutes . . . by that time I was going to burst. "Oh well, I'm just going to pee myself," I said. I didn't have a choice. But I was still waiting for someone to come in. When a CNA finally came in, after sitting in my own urine for thirty minutes, she had a big mess to clean up. Then she acted like it was all my fault. I didn't argue with her. There was no point. I didn't care. I was just relieved to get out of that chair. I will never go through that again.

Joan and Ashly came to visit a few days later. I was happy to see them and pretty much needed them to be there. Who wouldn't want their friends there in times of need? We caught up on our lives and stuff. I felt like I was in a different place and didn't care about all the things that happened to me here. None of that mattered. I was just happy to spend time with them. Everything was great until they started telling me, "You're a strong person," "You're brave to go through all this for your mom and brother," "You're an inspiration to us all," and blah, blah, blah. I hate when people say those things about me. I know that's a good thing but not for me. I let them go on and on and didn't want to be rude.

Then David came in to visit as well. We were all talking about everything and out of nowhere Joan said and did something I would never forget. She told David, "I did this to Peter's heart." The worst part of it was as she was saying that, she held up her hand and made a fist with a cracking sound. She was jokingly laughing afterwards. Right in front of me. David and I looked at each other stunned and shocked. We both were thinking the same thing. "Did she really do that?" I said silently to David. He nodded. "Why would she do that to me?" while thinking to myself. I was already broken to the ground from being stuck at this place. *"Does she want to make it worse or what?"* while in deep thought. She thought that it was funny. We didn't think it was. I don't think she even knew what she had done. After they left, David and I both said, "What the hell was that?" After that, I decided that I won't draw strength from love like that again. I didn't have anything left to hold onto. "What else can possibly go wrong?" I asked. "Don't jinx yourself," David replied.

I was counting the days that I will leave this horrible place. Three more days to go. The next day, the doctor wanted another sputum test to see if I still had pneumonia. It turned out to be negative. "Yay," I said. In a few more days, I'll be at a better place called Angel View. David was right. I did jinx myself. He came in later that day. I didn't think anything was wrong so I was asking him about Angel View. "Just three more days," I said to him. "Well, I got a call from Terri," he said. She said, "Can you tell Peter for me, that he can't come yet? I can't bear to tell him the bad news." "Why didn't she tell me herself?" I asked. "Well, she's a sissy. And she sounded like she was in tears," he said as he laughed. "That's not funny," I said. "Why can't I go yet?" I asked. I was curious. "Well, the bed hasn't opened up yet. The resident that you will replace is waiting for a bed at another Angel View home," David explained. "How long?" I wondered. "Ten days. Sorry," he said. I don't have a choice but to wait another ten days.

I was counting the days again. One day . . . two days . . . three days . . . four days . . . seven days later, I was coughing a lot and my secretion was changing colors from clear to green to yellow. I tested again and the doctor found out that my pneumonia had returned. I guess what Terri had said when she visited me had come true. When David came in, I told him. He said Angel View won't take me until the pneumonia is cleared. I had ten days of antibiotics to take. David called Terri about my reoccurrence of pneumonia. "Dang, almost made it," I said disappointedly. It's common in these places to get pneumonia again.

As I finished the last of the antibiotics, David had told me that Terri will take me in four days. I was excited. So I waited and waited. Two days later, David came in and I knew something was up. I asked him, "I'm not going in two days, am I? And Terri couldn't tell me, either?" "Nope," he shook his head. "What is her excuse this time?" I asked. "She couldn't get an Angel View bus to pick you up," as he laughed. I stuck my tongue at him. "Wow David, four days became four weeks," I mentioned. "Sorry, I didn't know this would happen. You can handle another week," he said. "Easy for you to say. You're not the one lying here," I said looking away. It wasn't his or Terri's fault—just my luck.

As usual, I was counting down the days. Just two more days, I thought, but then David came in and said, "Guess what?" "I'm going to get out of here?" I said sarcastically. "Nope," he said. So I just lift my hand up a bit and flipped him off. He laughed. "What is it this time?" I asked. "Well, this time she didn't have a nurse to come get you," he said laughing. I asked him, "Why would I need a nurse to come get me?" "It's one of Angel View's policies that a resident must have a nurse just in case the resident needs a treatment or something happens to the ventilator, so they won't die. Hahaha," he said. "I might as well live here," I said. It was going to take another week. "Why can't they get me the next day?" I asked him. He said that AV doesn't admit new clients on Fridays or the weekends.

A week was almost up. I wasn't expecting that I was going to AV anytime soon. David comes in shaking his head. "Getting my hopes up," I said. He shook his head. At this point I wasn't disappointed at all. "What's the excuse this time?" I asked David. He replied, "You have the worst luck." I nodded. "The street where the house is on is being worked on," David said shaking his head. I told him that I may be a strong-willed person but there's a limit to what I can take. I won't be able to take much more of this. I didn't sign up for this. "Just shoot me," I blurted out loud. David said, "I just might if they don't take you the next time. Or I'll just take you there myself. Just one more week," he mentioned. "I'll believe it when it happens. No point of counting the days. It won't happen. I'll just take my Ativan and be a junkie again," I said with a small grin.

## January 24, 2007

At last, the day finally came with good news. David told me that I was going to Angel View. "Terri will get you there tomorrow. Whatever it takes, she said." "Finally, I can get out of here," I said with a smile. I was anxious all night and didn't get any sleep.

David said, "There were many letdowns: with the pneumonia, with Angel View, with your daily care, and especially with Joan and Ashly. They began to distance themselves from you, you who wanted their friendship so badly; the reality of their departure from your life was heavy and best pushed back down deep where you used to store thoughts of trachs and facilities and death. But, thanks to Joan's great demonstration of how she crushed your heart, you moved through this pain too. Each day I visited for all those days at the San Bernadino subacute, you pulled yourself back together physically, emotionally, and you decided to give this 'new' life of yours a shot."

**January 25, 2007**

I woke up the next morning hoping I wouldn't get any bad news again. The discharge planner came in told me what was going to happen to me. I was told that I would be discharged at ten o'clock in the morning but I would have to wait for Pulmocare to set up my ventilator to take to AV. They are a respiratory company that can provide me with all my equipment. Then I would be taken to AV by ambulance. The CNA came in and got me ready. The nurse came in afterwards and took off my IV line and my G-Tube feeding. I was all ready to go. Now I have to wait.

It was 8:30 am when Pulmocare came. They had my ventilator with them. It was an LP 10 model. It was gray and white. It was just a big block. I was thinking, "Where in the world am I going to put that thing?" They began to take out gadgets and more tubing. "How many more tubes do I need to have? Jeez," I said to myself. I asked them questions about the use of each of the equipment. Well, I need to understand how my ventilator works. "Who's in charge of your health?" David says to me all the time. I finally understood what each setting of the ventilator, equipment and tubes do. There was so much to learn but I got it down. It's my own life, here. I may one day have to tell people how to troubleshoot my ventilator if anything were to happen. The LP 10 ventilators are very simple to learn because there aren't any electronics to deal with. There were knobs to turn for each setting. They finished setting up my ventilator and now they're going to switch me over on the LP 10. It was weird at first and I was telling them how each setting wasn't adjusted to my comfort. I told them what was wrong and the RT would adjust the settings accordingly. I was all set and suddenly the EMT arrived to take me to Angel View.

It was time to go. The EMT didn't know how to put my ventilator and me on the gurney. So they just put the ventilator between my legs. I was still in my gown and three blankets. I took my pillow with me that I got from the ICU. As I was being wheeled out to the ambulance, I told all the nurses and CNAs, "Thank you for taking care of me." I didn't want to be rude and say something bad. And they want me to visit after I settled in. "Yeah right, I would never visit again." When I got out to the parking lot, I said, "I'm out of here. Wow, it's cold out here." I felt a great relief. Pulmocare went on ahead to set up my equipment at Angel View.

Going to Angel View will take forty-five minutes to get to; it is located in Desert Hot Springs, California. Looking out the window, I realized that in the subacute my spirit was hitting rock bottom. Every day I was there, I felt myself disappearing from the reality of never getting out of there. I finally understood why I was able to survive my ordeal. It was my mom and David. If it wasn't for them for coming every night, I don't know how bad it would have been. I might have given up on everything and shut down. I am fortunate enough to have a loving mother who worked all day and my best friend/brother, David, who came every night to see me and made me feel comfortable there. I am grateful for them.

We drove into town, I didn't see anything, mostly houses. We drove to the main office and found out that we had to go to one of Angel View's nineteen homes. The staff gave them directions to the Jack Surnow House. We were on our way. When I arrived and came out of the ambulance, and saw a few staff outside waiting for me. I was wheeled in my room. There were no hallways, just a big open area to roll around and I saw two bathrooms, one big and one half the size of the other. One side of the wall is blue and others are white. And there was a ceiling fan. I was like, "Wow." My bed was next to the window. After I was transferred onto my bed, I saw my TV, computer, desk and all these pictures of my family on the shelf of my desk. My TV was a flat screen and hung up on top of my computer desk. Apparently my dad had built a TV stand connected behind and on the top of the desk. That TV will be the only thing standing if an earthquake happens. It was a nice setup. As I looked over to my left, I have a roommate. He looked like he was living but not in there. He was going to be a great roommate, I thought to myself. The Surnow House staff came in one at a time to introduce themselves.

# 10. Depression

At first, I was asking myself, "What have I gotten myself into?" Something wonderful, as it turns out. But it didn't seem like it then. A few days later, I was in my new room on my computer looking at all the pictures of my family and friends on my desk. My life changed completely. I sat there and I felt that I lost everything: my family, friends, and my life that I had at home. I was wondering, "What's the point of going on if I have the feeling that I lost everything important to me?" I've also told myself that maybe I regret getting the tracheotomy. There was so much negativity and very dark thoughts going through my head. I kept telling myself that I'm going on and living here for my mom and my family. So in a way, this decision to keep going is influenced by my living surroundings. But when it came down to it, it was my decision alone to make. I wasn't being brave or courageous for continuing to live longer.

The living surrounding is completely different from what I had imagined when this stage of my life came. I always imagined that I'll be living at home the rest of my life. I didn't expect having a tracheotomy would be so complicated. I felt that I was thrown away and not needed anymore. I miss my family. I was not prepared for this change in my life. My mind was still on the subacute with the horrible experiences. I've known that a transition of a great change would be very difficult. It was getting to me and I just sat there in my room looking at my family pictures and I just cried. I shook my head and said, "Dang it." I was more miserable than before. I was sad and felt unsafe because I still had anxiety about the subacute.

I was stuck at a crossroad in my mind. I kept falling and falling. I didn't want to adapt to my new life. I kept shaking my head, regretting that I've made this decision. I can't take back my decision. I hated it. I can honestly say that I've lost myself and ended up not caring to adapt to my current living situation. I closed my heart off completely. I didn't have the strength or will to get past my darkness on my own. No one noticed that I was going through that. I kept telling myself I'm doing this for my mom and brother, Jason. David told me, "In six months when you get a bit heavier, you'll see. It's going to get better. If not, we can figure out what to do next. Trust me," he said. I said, "Okay."

The next couple of days, I had a clearer mind than at the subacute. The Registered Nurse, Barney Riggs, at the time was passing my medications through my G-Tube. He was at the last medication to give me and it happened to be a laxative called Lactulose. He's a good nurse but he talks and talks and talks. I looked at it and told him, "I don't want that. It's going to be bad." He kept insisting that I need it. After a few minutes, I gave in. "Great," he said. He was so happy about it, with a big smile. Must have been exciting for him . . . geez, it was only a laxative. "You won't be sorry," he said. I gave him a dirty look. There goes my Lactulose down my G-Tube, a dark orange color. An hour later, my stomach started rumbling and started to hurt. Then I just looked up and shook my head. I was sweating bullets trying to hold it but I couldn't. I did my thing and thought the feeling was gone. Boy, was I wrong. I was miserable and suffering from my stomach turning all day. I went to the toilet eight times that day; so exhausting. Barney had to help put me on the toilet each time. At least it cleaned out my colon. The following day, Terri and the Director of Nurses gave him a lecture. I missed it. I was initiated into Surnow House with laxative.

I didn't really know anything about my roommate. He was very quiet and didn't really move. The staff told me about him. He never talked and made a few noises but he never bothered me. I don't know if he was in there. I hope he wasn't. Being stuck like that, I don't want to live like him. That's no life at all. I did everything I wanted to the room but I always respected his stuff and space. I always hated Saturdays because his mom would visit and to be polite and respectful of their time together, I would give them the room to themselves for the whole visit. I was so bored on Saturdays but I know I could stay in the room while she visits. She was reading to him and playing the radio, and basically taking care of him with certain things. It's only once a week. Every time I would leave, I would see my roommate making a grin at me for leaving him with his mom. I just grab my mp3 player and listened to my music while pacing around the house.

I live with five other guys with Muscular Dystrophy. We are all in the same boat. We make the best of it. It's like a dorm where some days some residents act up; some days are quiet; some days are funny; some days someone is sad; some days some are fighting with one another but it's all good. It's never a dull moment. Like a big happy family at the end of the day.

I needed someone or others to give me some light or to reassure me my decision was right for me, even if it's just a tiny bit. I'm certain that that "light" will come from someone that I know. I didn't know anyone here (except Terri and David). I didn't know her, but I've only met her once at the subacute. I didn't know she drops by the house all the time. David continued to drop by twice a week since he's AV's Occupational Therapist Consultant. He came twice a week to help me with the transition from home to AV. He assured me that living here will be better for me.

Since David can't be here 24/7, Terri made me feel safe without any anxiety over staff care I was getting. She'll do something if I have any complaints. Kindness can go a long way to help others. I can honestly say that I did lean against her kindness. Her kindness helped me. My thoughts of being here have changed because of that. Simply "just being present" ("The Uncertainty Principle") was the biggest reason for me to feel safe here. It's a very difficult reason to find because little reasons are always passed by. "Observation is a more powerful force than you could possibly reckon. The invisible, the overlooked, and the unobserved are those that are most in danger of reaching the end of the spectrum. They lose the last of their light. From there, anything can happen" ("The Uncertainty Principle"). It's not much but the significance of "just being present" is very meaningful and powerful. I'm grateful to Terri and David for just being there for me. They changed my heart, mood, outlook, reasons, and thoughts about living here with a tracheotomy.

My life, or anyone's, makes a difference to everyone around them, big or small. People may not feel or see it but it's there. "Just being present" can make a difference for anyone. People don't realize that the people we encounter can give them something or anything. We won't see it given or passed on to them. What do you think may be given, you asked? We can't really see what was given unless we are very observant, but we still have to feel it. The act of just being there can give someone hope, life, energy, inspiration, happiness, a sense of being needed, dreams, motivation, love or any emotions that I may miss. And of course, all the bad emotion too. Nonetheless, it's still making a difference, no matter how significant or insignificant it may be.

After a few months of living here at AV, my mom came to visit once every two weeks. As she started to see that I was healthy and gaining some weight, she came less and less. I was okay with it; I didn't mind it because I don't want her to drive so far to visit me. When I go home to visit my mom or attend a birthday party, I noticed a big change in my mom; she looked so rested, relaxed, and happy. I have not seen that from her in ages. I sensed a huge burden had lifted from her shoulders. Mom isn't so worried about me living here. She's very happy to see me living and smiling again. A great relief of being a heavy burden on my mom had lifted from my heart when I first saw my mom like that.

Joan and Ashly came to visit a few times from Orange County. The few times Joan was here, my feelings for her were still there and I couldn't stop thinking about her. That day, I made a choice to want to get better and to move on or I will always be stuck in that moment. I know it's not healthy, and I feel it. But then they stopped visiting. I decided to just cut Joan out of my life completely. I told Ashly that I would keep in touch with her but I also told her that I do not want to talk about Joan or to know what she's doing or how her life is going. She said, "Okay." This is the only way I know how to move on and to start living again. Angel View is my new life now. After a few weeks later, I felt relieved. It took a new scenery for me to move on, starting over.

What I realized from them not visiting anymore is that friends will come and go and I would have to make new friends along the road of life. I shouldn't be frustrated or upset about friends leaving without even noticing. I told myself to make friends no matter where I go, with every opportunity. When do people like me get a chance to meet people? It's not like we can go out "just because." When friends start a family, they will concentrate on their families, not the friendship. This way I won't feel the bad emotional feelings and be able to move on. Life begins for them; family or career. I have to expect that and just go out and meet people, making more friends to make up for lost ones. That's all I can do.

David told me that if I worked on getting fatter to be comfortable sitting all day, he would take me to my aunt's wedding, and out on adventures. He told me to find out what needs to be done to take me out. I said okay. I asked around and he needed to be trained with my ventilator. He told me to schedule it. And of course I did. The Registered Nurse does the training. It usually takes an hour to learn. David had to learn my ventilator settings, how to troubleshoot the ventilator; how to change an inner cannula and a trach; learn to use an Ambu bag and how to use the portable suction machine. It took me six months to get fat: forty pounds heavier. David has taken me everywhere and through him, I'm experiencing the saying, "just live." He is giving up his free time to take me everywhere to enjoy the meaning of the word *life*.

We've been to the Tram in Palm Springs and we went down the mountain and the dirt trail until I got stuck. It was cold and we went back up the mountain to get on the last tram ride down the mountain. I didn't want to stay up there all night. We also went to Las Vegas for a few days to meet up with David's two brothers. We went to the Blue Man group show. It was funny and I enjoyed it. Then David lost me at the Stratosphere on the top. He stopped to look at something and I kept going, looking out the window. How could he lose me from a circle? He stopped and waited for me to come around again. All good. He also has used me as a guinea pig to help teach one of Dr. Heather Thomas' Occupational and Dr. Bonnie Forrester's Physical Therapy class at Loma Linda University.

[The microphone please! David Erickson, OT and I enter the classroom. We are teaching a "wheelchair" class to the Occupational Therapy students here at Loma Linda University. The microphone is a wireless lapel mic for me, I want my snappy responses to David's sarcasm well understood! "Can you hear me now?" I'm his wingman. With handouts passed around, "Let's get started," David said; yikes, there are so many eyes upon us. The toughest hour of this lecture had begun; blah, blah, blah. Of course David talked, bounced pages/papers all over the place. I said, "Everyone notice: ADHD in action." The students looked stunned, they had heard me say that, my newly amplified whisper. "Oops, you guys were not supposed to hear that," I said. Keeping David on his feet by making sarcastic comments to keep the students alert is part of my "job." Finally, the first hour is over . . . phew. Everyone takes a five minute break to stretch their legs. "Ooh, you mean I can get up and stretch?" I ask. The students laugh. Next, David talks about a part of my chair and I demonstrate it. I am a wheelchair model (no, I don't do swimsuit modeling). I demonstrated how my chair reclines, tilts, etc. Then, I need a cannula change, but, the lecture must go on. David attended to me, while Dr. Forrester, PT, took over. Students clapped as we finished the class; Kaitlynn Grant said "It makes more sense to be able to visualize it," Irene Lee said, "We learned how to take measurements while watching real life demonstrations. I never thought it could be so enjoyable!" And lastly Sarah Thomas said, "Peter's wit and charm made studying wheelchairs fun. The bantering back and forth between Peter and David was priceless and had our entire class cracking up!"]

It's a way for me to give back to them and to meet new people and to make new friends. We talk about my power chair, Muscular Dystrophy, my ventilator and my daily life. The students learn more with visuals, a prop, like me.

It's like David teaching me about life through his eyes and heart. I get to experience pieces of his own experiences through his words. "See your life for what it is, and escape from your cage. You may find a completely different world out there" (*Fatal Fury*). Pieces of life were kept hidden from me by Muscular Dystrophy (MD), the invisible cage. He was trying to teach me that there is so much out there that I could do regardless of having MD. I was never strong enough to experience life, or was too afraid to do so. But he also taught me in a different way that I had to work on. I had to be able to observe his actions to better myself, to see the positive side of life, and to have a heart because MD and life had turned my heart cold. When you teach others in your own way or if it just comes out, and if they take it to heart, you are actually passing pieces of your teaching on to them. You won't realize it and neither will they. I have felt his teachings and have acted out without realizing it. Making a difference. What better thing to do for others? It's free, unseen and willingly given. No one asks for it. So in a way, we are being taught through others. This cycle is never ending, transferring knowledge through others.

I can honestly say that David is my best friend. Throughout all my friends, none were ever my best friend. I was never able to hang out with anyone. Everything was complicated around me. I dealt with my feelings toward all that when "friends" would disappear from my life. I wasn't interesting enough to hang out with. I felt that I wasn't needed or belonged to. They say they want to but it never happens. I never knew what it was like to have a best friend until I got trached and ventilated. I never allowed myself to go out or to experience life.

David stepped in and offered to take me around everywhere to experience life outside of home. I felt a burden from my heart disappearing for wanting to go and experience life. I didn't feel I was making someone take me places; David wanted to. I've been experiencing life with each opportunity given. I've done more with David than I ever had in the twenty-one years before we met. He's always there when I need him and always giving me his time.

I wish I can do things for him like giving him some of my time. I wish he would ask me for more of my time because he's always giving his, or count on me as I count on him. He hasn't disappeared from my life. I felt I belong finally. But sometimes, I wonder if I'm taking his time for granted. I can't make any excuses if I am; maybe because I don't have any barriers up now. If I am, I hope he gets on me about that, so I can re-evaluate myself to stop myself from being like that even if it takes years to make that change. I do not want him to disappear from my life like most of my friends did.

I know I want to build my character to be like his; he does teach me in his own way by using his actions. And I pick up on his character to be close to his as I can. I know I may never have a character like his but I can try to reach it. What I'm saying is that I look up to him and he inspires me to do better things with what I've got—to be human.

To sum it all up, David is a very selfless man, a mentor, and *"a man of much substance as grace"* (Three Rivers). He is one of the good persons of this world who always gives his time, effort and even his money to the less fortunate. He's only one man that I know that tries to make a difference for the disabled, not for the whole world, but to the few that are reachable. I've known him for more than fifteen years now and I still can't really define him. But I can say that he's been there for me through all the hardships and trials I've been through. More importantly, I can honestly say and finally realized that he became more than my best friend; he became a part of my family. He became one of my brothers. I hope he sees me as one of his brothers.

One day, Dave Thornton (Angel View Executive Director) called me up last minute and asked if I would like to be on a radio talk show, The Joey English Show. I didn't think anything of it and said, "Yes. Do I get a free lunch?" He said, "Sure." I soon realized that I have never done anything like that before. It also hit me that I'm not good at talking to new people I meet. I get very nervous; I freeze a bit; I stutter, and all that. It's even worse than when I do a speech for a class. Now let alone, it's a live radio show. Too late for me to change my mind. I told myself, "Just get it over with." I got my nurse (Karen Korman) to get me ready and ten minutes later, my transportation had arrived. I didn't even have a chance to change. We set off going to the CBS2 TV Station out in Thousand Palms. It was about twenty to thirty minute drive from my house. It was out of nowhere, just more sand. Dave met me there. He was waiting at the entrance. I followed him into the studio. We walked into a TV set and I thought it was a radio talk show. This was my first time at a TV station. It was what I had expected from a studio. I was waiting on the sidelines and I noticed the wall closest to me. It had a lot of names autographed. There were a few celebrity names that I recognized. The producer came up to me and handed me a sharpie. I autographed the wall.

I had to wait to go on stage. The first guest was a local pharmacist. My nurse chickened out. She didn't want to go on stage with me. I got left hanging out there. Some wing girl I got. I said, "You big chicken." "Yeah, I know," she replied. I told her, "Okay, you just sit there." I stuck my tongue at her as I got on stage. I didn't know what to expect. All the lights shining on me . . . Joey English gave me a few tips about being on camera. "Don't look at the cameras and just answer my questions looking at me, like in any conversation, and you'll be fine," she said. "Yeah right," I said. I did what she said and gosh, I was so nervous and sweating. I stuttered a few times. The biggest thing I messed up on was that Joey English asked, "What do you like to do for fun?" Stupid me—I blew it on local TV and said, "I like to roll around the house." I had an opportunity to get a donated van for myself to visit my family and hang out with friends more often. But I blew it. Dave Thornton walked me out of the station to the bus, he gave me twenty-three dollars for lunch. I went to In-N-Out. I got my free lunch. What an experience to face. It was horrible. But it was a good experience to learn from. I didn't know it yet but this was a stepping stone for me.

After the TV interview, Dave always asked me to go with him to speak at schools, different Rotary Clubs of the desert, newspaper interviews and attend Angel View events. I have never turned him down on any of his invites. I wouldn't give up any opportunities to practice with my speaking in public. What better way to practice speaking than in front of a mirror? I have to learn the hard way even if it was bad or not. It also helped me conquer my fear of speaking on stage in front of a crowd and being in front of the cameras. And best of all, meeting new people. I'm having fun doing it too. A lot of doors opened up for me from that fateful day. I realized that if I had said no to Dave that day, I believed he would not asked me anymore and that would be it.

I have written an article about one of my Rotary Club speaking engagements.

On June 23, 2011, Dave Thornton, Brenda Vosbein (my nurse) and I walked to the conference room of the Aqua Soleil Hotel and Spa to speak with the Desert Hot Springs Rotary Club. I looked around, I said to Dave, "There is no microphone. Look here, I brought my voice amplifier." "Great," he said. The club members started coming in, Dave and I discussed a game plan with our speech. Members greeted one another, friends close and far, and lunch got under way. The president rang the bell to start. We started off with the Pledge of Allegiance of the

USA and the Rotary Club pledge. Everyone began eating, but it was time for Dave and me to speak. My nurse helped set up my voice amplifier while Dave gave the opening lines, "What better way to talk about Angel View than to have a client speak about their experiences to you guys instead of me," Dave said. I worked from what was said. Dave and I switched off speaking. I would throw in some of my sarcasms for laughs. Dave spoke more on Angel View in general while I spoke about Angel View as a resident and included my life background. I spoke mainly about my mom and how I came to be at Angel View. "Moving to Angel View lifted a great burden from my mom," I said. I made one member cry from my words. It really touched her heart. Afterwards, we stayed over and answered questions. I really wanted to finish my lunch but missing the rest of my lunch was a small price to pay to share a part of my story to anyone who wants to listen. Afterwards, I talked with one of its members, Bruce Craven. He is the Program Director of the Columbia Advanced Management Program for Colombia Business School. I answered all his questions. He emailed me with his response from my visit.

[Statement from Bruce Craven: "On June 23, 2011 at the Aqua Soleil Hotel in Desert Hot Springs, I had the pleasure of listening to Peter speak about his positive experience as a guest at the Angel View's facility. He also spoke about his personal approach to managing his physical disability, with a focus on his larger goal of maximizing his intellectual engagement, his productivity and pleasure in life.

As someone that works in two different fields: executive education for the Columbia Business School and, on occasion, in the entertainment industry as a writer, I was struck by the clarity and optimism with which Peter approached his physical limitations. He explained to me after the talk that he had a simple choice, either to whine and be a victim or to take control of his environment and use his energy to be creative and to inspire and mentor others, including his younger brother. I have seen very successful people, unhindered by physical limitations, get derailed by their emotions and their negativity, often causing them great pain and leading them down a path of helplessness and frustration. This has happened to me personally and it was inspiring to hear Peter's simple and courageous approach to confronting his challenges. He leads himself to operate from a position of confidence, humor and commitment. He makes this choice consciously and explains his choice in simple, effective language.

In my work in executive education, one challenge that global executives embrace is taking responsibility for their situation in life—professionally and personally—and accepting the obligation to improve that situation. I have watched people from all around the business world work hard to prepare to be more effective leaders. I have seen changes in these individuals that have positively impacted themselves and the people they lead. Last Thursday, at our local Rotary in Desert Hot Springs, I listened to Peter and spoke with him afterwards about his approach to his challenges. To some degree, I work in the business of helping to inspire others, yet Peter inspired me and left me eager and excited to go back and take his guidance into my personal and private life and work to improve myself.]

# 11. Life

## Falling In Love Again

I fell in love again, with a girl name Karin. What do I feel about all this from her? It's been a few weeks and I've been searching for answers inside my heart. Yes, I found the answers I saw within myself and it wasn't easy but was painful. I wasn't as strong as I thought because the pain almost completely took over my heart. I feel that I'm losing her. In my heart, I feel that my heart is just open, with no bottom. More like my heart is open but it's really not. I didn't really do anything with her. I was just being myself, trying to help her so she can see me and not the wheelchair.

We are all connected to each other in one way or another. Connections aren't necessarily seen or physically felt. We will never physically connect with everyone but it's there. They are invisible. A connection can be any form or substance; from: a smile, a touch, a choice, a brief encounter, a moment, a glance, a left click of a mouse, listening to the radio, watching a movie or TV show, a hello, a goodbye, a greeting, a text, a chain letter, an email, Facebook (yes, Facebook), emotions, through a friend, and choices. Basically, a connection can be created from an infinite numbers of ways. No matter how insignificant to important connections are, they're still connections.

Connections influence the choices we have to choose from. Unique choices that each person gets are theirs and only theirs. "A thousand fibres connect you with your fellow-men, and along those fibres, as along sympathetic threads, run your actions as causes, and return to you as effects. (Henry Melvill). Choices are also connections which affect everyone not only you.

> "We all struggle to find the right path to take in life. It's not always easy to know what that is or where it will lead us. In the end, it's the people in our lives that provide us the balance to help us make it through." (*Kyle XY*)

Connections are formed before we are born. We don't realize that connections are happening throughout time. Throughout time, connections were being created from everyone having a tiny connection with one person to another and so on. Every connection made passed on from one person to the next and to the next. We pass each connection we encountered on to others. Connections started with our ancestors to get to the point in time of our birth. "Life is a puzzle. Every connection fits together to create who we are, what we do, how we feel. Every connection that creates an experience shapes us into who we eventually will become" (*Kyle XY*).

A person that lives across the world has a connection with another on the opposite side of the world even if they have never met. How, you ask? The connections we create for good or bad will create another connection, and that in turn another, until who knows where it stops or in what far place our connections will be created.

Karin and I were connected before we even met one another by the connections of others. People make connections to connect us together. We don't know who influences these connections to a certain point of time of our meeting. "The briefest connection can make the strongest, most indelible impression. Sometimes, the connections you make with other people sneak up on you. You share experiences. You have a history. You form a bond" (*Kyle XY*). We have that from one little connection that connected to us more ways than one. Who knows how many connections are needed to connect us together? The power of connections.

"Each contact with a human being is so rare, so precious, one should preserve it" (Anais Nin 2). In a way, connections are preserved throughout the connections of dots of the world. Connections touch people in a bad or good way depending on the last dot to connect with you. Some are lucky and some are not. Some become rich and some are poor. Some are healthy and some are sick. Some experience love and some are teased by love.

"Rain will fall and storms will come but the scenery continues to change, and if left alone, it will be forever." (*Rozen Maiden*)

Continue to reach out for connections and you'll eventually encounter a connection that can change everything for the best.

"My tears were coming to an end. My heart is finally able to dance for joy again. I know someday the sadness will fade away. The pain I felt then will be nothing more than a memory. I know it's okay to cry until that time comes. It's okay to stop sometimes while I wash everything away with tears. I thought so many times that I can't take it anymore. I've thought about giving up and just throwing in the towel. When I was down and looked up toward the sky, a connection was formed to brighten a path for tomorrow. Everyone must bear their own burdens. I bet this is just our personal trials. It's these hard times that will make me stronger." (*Naruto Shippûden The Movie: Bonds*)

A connection made will change one's life for the best or for the worst. No one knows. We just have to believe that that connection will come to us sooner than later. I was waiting for a very long time for that connection to catch up to me.

"Everyone were the main cast for each of these 'Every days.'" (*Blue Drop*)

Being disabled with Muscular Dystrophy and not being selfish, is such a lonely life when it comes down to love. Going through and dealing with a heartbreak have changed me or anyone for the worse. I know; I've been through it. The heartbreak I have experienced taught me powerful lessons on the kind of love I really want to experience. I realized that it's just a big disappointment and that I'm being cheated. Sometimes I wish that I couldn't love, fall in love or want love. Maybe I should have remained bitter about it all and not shown my heart. I couldn't cry for anything afterwards and my heart was cold and mean toward love. My heart hardened so much because of love that my tears dried up completely. But I was wrong.

I thought I was strong enough to handle love without having any chance of experiencing love from another. I was doing pretty well. I expected that there wouldn't be a chance for me anyway.

"The mind has a thousand eyes. And the heart but one; Yet the life of a whole life die when love is done." (Francis William Bourdillon)

When I met Karin that day—"I wonder just how many times a miracle like that occurs in the world at that same moment. There are some nights I feel like crying because I feel that I may not have a place in her future" (*Bluer Than Indigo*).

"Everyone should carefully observe which way his heart draws him, and then choose that way with all his strength." (Hasidic Saying)

"Kindness in words creates confidence. Kindness in thinking creates profoundness. Kindness in giving creates love." (Lao Tzu)

I want to tell her, "Love will enter cloaked in friendship's name" (Ovid). And all of a sudden, love started entering my heart again. I wasn't planning on chasing love again.

I'm feeling this way because I found out about her feelings toward me and I did not expect that kind of a response from her. I got more than what I wanted to know.

It turns out that she does have feelings toward me. I figured out that much already. I knew she liked me that way but never to the extent of what I found out. But there were other things mentioned that made me speechless and in awe. She's stuck in the middle between her ex-boyfriend and me. She was asked, "Who would you choose between the two?" she said, "I would pick you. Because you're easy to talk to. He's normal, understanding and very caring toward me." She was also asked, "Who would you marry if you had to pick?" She picked me. I was surprised and speechless. I guess another client's saying might be right after all, "Peter and Karin are getting married on the beach." But then again she mentioned my MD that was getting in the way. I know that she's the closest one that I can honestly say would say yes toward me.

I'm being selfish but if she still does after she understands, then I won't feel liked I cheated her of love and everything else that comes with love that I won't be able to do for her. I won't deny myself of love if this condition was met.

All I can do is to see how this will turn out. I won't hope, pray or wish for it. "Wishes won't be granted just by thinking about them," (School Days). I will not allow myself to get my hopes up. I cannot deal with false hope on this anymore. Being around people all the time won't change the fact that love is selfish. I believe in her with "tomorrow's tomorrow" (Ladner).

For the first time in my life, I finally met someone who actually feels the same way about me. I was truly enjoying life again. I felt happy, really I was. I was laughing; I was able to joke around; make friends; meet people and not lying about who I am to everyone. She was the reason why I was able to heal my heart. I started falling for her more and more. I told her how I feel about her and she gave me a response. It wasn't toward my favor, after all that. "Destiny is the bridge you build to the one you love" (My Sassy Girl). No matter how much I give her from caring, to loving her, I still fell short, very short. She had the same feelings toward me and I wasn't the one she picked.

She went back to her ex. There are always two sides of love. People think it's a great thing but never realize how much pain it can create. I can't blame her because it was her choice anyway. It was always her choice. Choices we make affect everyone, not just ourselves. There are always two paths for each choice made.

She wants me to stay the same but I can never be the same again. That's impossible. People change from enduring pain or from love. "One of the hardest things in life is to watch the one you're in love with, be in love with someone else" (Anonymous).The distance between us will become farther and farther apart. I feel that I don't have the right to be around in her life. I feel like, "What's the point?" Pain and more pain? Being her friend, I can't do much for her. I have limits. Things I want to say to her but can't.

She said, "Thanks for understanding." How am I supposed to respond to that? I said that because I feel that I'm always the one who has to understand other people's feelings, but what about my feelings for once? People expect me to always do what's right for another because I'm a nice guy. People think I'm a strong person because I don't let anything get to me. I'm not a strong person like everyone believes. I'm just as vulnerable like everyone else with love. People don't realize that I'm only strong when I'm in love or being with another.

Love isn't fair. It was never fair to begin with. Love is the most selfish emotion in the universe. This just makes me believe that love is fake. And love doesn't exist. It's not love; it's what we can do for each other. Life sucks without love. Love can't overcome anything.

All this may or may not happen depending on the choices she makes. Only time will tell because she might change her heart toward me. "I wish you were a story with a happy ending and the wisdom to look for it" (*My Sassy Girl*).

Deep down in my heart, I feel that she won't choose me. It's a big waste of time like most people had said. Why am I the one in the background of her life? Why? Because she rarely hangs out with me. It's like we only hang out through texting. Maybe to her, I'm just someone she can turn to as the last resort. Am I on the end of her list? Why do I feel that I'm last? It shows in her actions.

Sometimes I wonder if she was just messing with my feelings. Does she keep me in her life to get advice or am I just a listener to her or am I just her shock absorber? I don't want to be her pet puppy and I don't want to be used either but it looks that way. She only comes to me when she needs something or to talk about her problems. There's always something blocking me from reaching the end. Is love just teasing me? If so, why even do this to her and me? Why do people say, "Tis better to have loved and lost than never to have loved at all" (Tennyson). That's not always true. Love can be the destroyer or death of someone. Love can be a sheath or the sharp end of the sword.

I believe that no one knows what will happen to us tomorrow. I try to live up to that belief. Sometimes it's a good thing and sometimes it's a bad thing. That is always a fifty/fifty chance I take when I'm like that. I stopped myself from playing the "what if" game and just take a step forward regardless of what happens. If this is love, than I must be a moron to think this way: Love can be a form of any kind of human emotion.

After all that, she told me why she wouldn't pick me. She said that she was only in her twenties and she was scared of the life with me. She talked about marriage, kids and a normal life. Then why would she even string me along for all these years. Argh! The next day, Karin ran away from my life. She changed all her contact information. She literally threw me away. I was so hurt that I wanted to change myself completely so I won't get hurt again.

> "Don't change who you are because some people are too stupid to appreciate it." (Terri Thompson)

Love sucks. Love doesn't exist. Love isn't real. Love is fake. Love is nothing more than what we can do for each other. I can't believe in love anymore. There's no reason to. It doesn't do anything for me. Love is a hurtful emotion. I don't want it anymore. The more I try, the more the pain inflicts my heart. Love is just using me. It only benefits others, never me. I will never open my heart again. The heart is weak and I won't gather any strength, inspiration, motivation, or anything from my heart again. I don't care anymore. I'll tell Cupid to just shoot himself. Keep his arrows to himself. Love is a big waste of energy. Love is so exhausting. I think love is just pulling my leg, teasing and laughing at me. Love isn't my strength but my greatest pain. Love isn't powerful. Hatred is. Why not go to the dark side? It won't hurt. Love is disappearing from me. I guess I'll start "hiding" again.

I mentioned all this to David and he gave me his honest answer about it. I could never get an answer like that from anyone that I can understand, except his.

## Advice From David

"Isn't it great to be human!

"Peter, Peter, Peter . . . Trust me, you will never give up on love. You can say it, you can write it down and you can repeat it every hour of every day, but when it comes along again you'll be there with your heart in your hand, ready to give it away.

"It's like childbirth. Ask a woman during her final hour of labor if she wants more kids. She'll say 'No way, this pain is killing me . . . I am so uncomfortable.' But ask her a year after that and she says, 'Yes, we are thinking of having another.'

"Time heals. What a cliche, but a true one.

"What you need to keep focused on is not to deny love, but to accept your life without it, and take what you get as a gift, not a NEED. If you don't NEED it, then when it comes along, even a flirt for a day, or a week, or whatever, it's a fun gift. It's fun to feel that love, but since you don't NEED it, it's an extra—NOT YOUR VERY LIFE.

"You've had too much pain, way too much. Focus on the moment. Don't give yourself away; don't give your heart away. Just have fun. You are a fun guy. You can love and have fun, without losing yourself along the way. It takes some focus and practice; try it, it works. "You give away your VERY LIFE every time, so that when love stumbles and fails, you want to die with it. Practice NOT giving up your life along with your heart next time. See it as 'fun,' a diversion from your normal feelings; something a bit extra BUT NOT NECESSARY. Don't give that love the power to own your heart, your very life."

I finally understand what I must do about love. I always said that I wasn't selfish but in reality I am. I was being selfish and I didn't realize it; changing who I am completely so that I won't hurt myself again. Giving up, to be exact; giving up from a great sadness, loss of a loved one, a great heartache. If I give up like that again, I'm being selfish to everyone around me. I made up my mind and just let her go . . . in three days.

I decided to follow his advice and not worry about wanting love. I just started focusing on life. Life will continue to move, no matter what.

I was thinking long and hard and came up with this saying: "Give up everything and let go." I came up with this from my experience with MD, experiencing, adapting to the changes and perspective of life through the eyes of MD. I have gone through the growing-up stage like any other MD individual, with all the disappointments, false hope, jealousy, dreams dying, and life disappearing right in front of my eyes. I started being pessimistic about everything first, expectations become ZERO. My quote means that in life, there's nothing changing, just more optimistic ideas that will bring forth high expectations with more disappointments, heartaches, jealousy, and regrets. Let go of optimism to live life without those emotions.

I was watching the clouds moving freely with the wind, any which way it wants. It had me thinking about dreams and life. Many have dreams which they want to come true. How many baskets of lemons will come out of the life many want to come true for themselves? Many want to make gallons and gallons of lemonade. As the clouds move faster away, I wonder how many of our dreams come and go. Many just see life passing them by, not getting many baskets of lemons they wanted. Life is life . . . many baskets of lemons or a basket with one lemon. I know I got a basket of one lemon—and it's okay. While dreams come and go, I'm still making gallons and gallons of lemonade with that one lemon. The point of this is, don't worry about how your life comes to be or how other people judge you on your life, or if it doesn't come out how you wanted; make it the best you can with the lemons you got. Life is worth enjoying to see the beauty the lemonade made.

People have called me Angel View's Poster Boy. I don't considered myself as one to begin with. Angel View provides so much for me to have a life here. Transportation: drivers, gas, maintenance; Necessities: water, electricity, food and other expenses, like medical stuff that insurance may not pay for; providing extra staff. I'm not doing anything at home anyway. I figured I can at least help out to give back. I know I can talk about my experiences and Angel View to others who want to listen, who want to donate, to the community and doing interviews, TV or newspapers. It's the least I can do for Angel View.

When Dave Thornton brought donors, potential donors or people to educate about Angel View to Surnow House, I was always the one giving the house tour. While giving the tours, I always use my personal story and experiences. It gives them a sense of realness. You can always give money but never see the realness of what the money is going toward. I do the tours because it's a way for me to talk to people and it's kind of fun.

David decided to give me a few of his available dates for the month to take me places to do whatever I want since he's already out here in the desert. So I decided to take Terri out to dinner. It was always fun around her and we became friends afterwards. A few times a year, I always invited her to dinner or when I couldn't find someone to go with. She was my backup date. We have eaten almost everywhere in the desert.

**Staff**

A life of Mondays . . . Direct Care Staff and Nurses can find themselves working any hour of any day of the week, crazy work schedules; and there are really no "holidays" or "weekends" off. They work every day because they care.

We are all stuck together in this house, in each other's business; even when we try and push each other away, we end up sharing in each other's lives. The good, the bad and the ugly. Privacy for staff and clients is often at a premium here. It is difficult to have your own space when everyone has access to it. Staff try and keep our lives personal, but it is difficult to do when they must have their hand in every part of it; since we are close with them, they are often sharing personal parts of their lives with us. We are really one big family.

Taking care of us, worrying about us, wiping our butts, cooking our dinner every night, helping us with everything we need. They're basically our hands. They do their best to meet our needs, protect our safety, and our well-being every day.

Many of us can't talk or are unable to tell them what we need; it's up to the staff to be our caregivers, housekeepers, psychologists, counselors, mind readers, facial and body expressions experts and being a loving parent, friend and worker. Loving parents will never get paid enough for what they go through and how much they have and will endure for their children. The staff do all this and more, and they do it for less. Many of us do not have any family support; either our families are too far away or, sadly, they just don't care. We need our staff and can't live without them.

Many staff have an amazing ability to observe and read non-verbal client's body language and eye movements to understand their personal needs. Sometimes I wonder if they are mind readers. That takes patience and the understanding and knowledge of a client's needs. Most staff are very devoted, with the unpaid duties that devotion brings to us; beyond dollars and benefits, and their immeasurable love and friendship to us clients, with qualities that can't be bought at any price. They do all this, often for clients who can't even voice a thank you. "The best and most beautiful things in the world cannot be seen or even touched—they must be felt with the heart" (Keller).

I've been asked to send in stories for the Angel View newsmagazine but I hadn't sent any in. One day I decided to send in a story for DeAnn Lubell, Angel View's Personal

Relations. I wondered what would happened if I just sent in a few. I kept writing for the newsmagazine, which comes out every quarter, and it wasn't too bad. Since I was the only one sending articles, she decided to give me my own page, called *Peter's Page*. "Ooh . . . my own page." Every time a newsmagazine came out, the staff would say, "Why are you on every page of the magazine?" I tell them, "I don't know. Hahaha . . . Probably because I get out there and do stuff." And they said, "It might as well be called *Peter's Newsmagazine*."

When I found out that Angel View has an annual luncheon with an Angel View Client of the Year and an Angel of the Year, I told Terri that I would not want to be one and if I have to, I'm taking her with me up on the stage. I got picked unanimously to be The Client of the Year of 2011. I said, "Okay." And the Angel of The Year was Barbara Sinatra. I said, "Ooh." I didn't really have to do anything, just take pictures with everyone and go up on stage to receive the award at the annual luncheon. That's what I was told. Then I was told that I was doing a photo shoot with Barbara Sinatra for the luncheon magazine. I never did a photo shoot before. First time for everything. It was held at The Barbara Sinatra Children's Center. I met Barbara there and I wasn't nervous or anything, thanks to all the interviews I've done. She was very nice. While we were waiting for the photographer to set up, Ms. Sinatra decided to give me a tour of her center. She told me the history of why she wanted to open this children's center. Like an indoor playground to help abused children, very awesome. It was time to start the photo shoot. We probably took a hundred photos. My mouth was hurting from smiling too much. It was so much fun though. She gave me some pointers for taking photos. There was an awesome shot of Ms. Sinatra and me looking into each other's eyes. She told me a tip to not strain my eyes from doing a shot like that, by just looking toward her and not look across and up.

Now she tells me. It was all good. Then we took a short break to rest our mouths. A few minutes later, someone else came in and I didn't know who she was. I introduced myself and she introduced herself as Robin Nelson. I still didn't know who she was. My first time meeting her. We resumed the photo shoot with Robin. It was awesome. They were really nice. Ms. Sinatra offered me water and stuff. I was good. I did ask for their autographs. They both gladly wrote their names on drink napkins. I wanted to make it look real like I just met them at a party or something. I came home and wrote Ms. Sinatra a thank you letter. And I had to Google who Robin Nelson was. I was impressed. That was it until the luncheon came. During the wait, I had to write a bio about myself for the speech at the luncheon, up on stage. I wrote one and I asked one of my good high school friends, René Aguirre, if he wanted to read it for me and to be my personal photographer. He said, "Okay." I didn't want to do it because of the ventilator; I can only say a few words before the ventilator cuts me off and I have to wait for a breath again.

Linda Kirch, an AV board member, kindly sponsored my whole table so that I can share this event with my family. Very nice of her. I invited my immediate family, David, René and Terri. I had to do my PR stuff before it started. I was greeting and thanking everyone and posing for the cameras with everyone, like a rock star. And I was also introducing my family to everyone.

After all the entertainment, Ms. Sinatra was honored first. She gave a speech and it was funny. She was given a nice plaque. I was called up to stage next with René to receive my award. It was a hard plastic star. Then René took the mic and gave my speech for me.

René says: "My name is René Aguirre. I have had the pleasure of knowing Peter for 20 years, since we were in high school together. Peter has asked me here today to speak on his behalf about his 'new' life since he got to Angel View four years ago. Peter asked the following people to stand up: (Many administration, staff and consultants stand; they stand up at once, as they have been told in advance to do so at this point in the speech: René waits as they stand.) Peter has told me that the people you see standing around you right now—these are some of the people that have given that extra little bit to make Peter's 'new' life here at Angel View not only tolerable, but special. Peter's body had failed him prior to coming to Angel View, but look around at those standing before you: these people have brought laughter and love into his heart here at Angel View. Being dependent on others for even the most simple or personal tasks is not something anyone wants for themselves, but Peter says that being here at Angel View has made his life a good one. It is an HONOR for him to accept the Client of the Year award today. Peter leaves us today with a quote by Italian writer Luciano de Crescenso, 'We are each of us Angels with only one wing; and we can only fly by embracing one another.' Peter thanks you, and I thank you. Good day."

My mom used to be embarrassed of my brother and me. She used to hide us from relatives and everyone. I never knew why until I told her that I'm going to start going to the family parties. She didn't object. And I realized why; every other relative always talked about how great their kids are and how successful they are and what college they graduated from and so on. My mom doesn't have any of that stuff to say with them. She feels sad about that and ashamed. I saw that for the first time. I didn't know what to say. She felt that way every time. They can do all that because they don't understand what my family goes through with two disabled kids at home. Stuck . . . a lot of sacrifices made for us. Finally I came to AV and all these opportunities opened up for me: on TV, my writings everywhere, on newspapers, magazines, and meeting people. Now she can tell them about me and all the stuff I'm doing. For the first time, my mom can be proud.

I have met so many interesting people along the way of my stay at Angel View. I met people from all walks of life.

February 08, 2013, I went to get my annual echocardiogram and cardiology follow up at Loma Linda University and Medical Center. The doctor showed me my results and my ejection fraction (a measurement of heart function) had improved. "Normal" is 50-65%, and mine went from 30% to 55%. "Ooh . . . I get to live a lot longer."

I could have easily let the weather make me gloomy and end up wasting a day of my life feeling down, but instead I took the rainbow—the brilliant and bright natural colors contrasted by the dark and gloomy skies. Out of the gloom came awe! I had a smile on my face. Then through the downpour of rain washing everything away, it was like life being swept clean with extremely cold temperatures and winds.

Later that night, I was shocked still. I had always thought my heart's ejection fraction could never improve with my diagnosis of Becker's Muscular Dystrophy; I'd only go downhill. But it improved; here was the proof in black and white. It could be from my great doctors and the new medications . . . and no, it's not a miracle.

Months later, I found out that my cardiac function was still at 30%. The 55% was a test mistake. I was devastated for an hour but I did learn a powerful lesson from this: "a breath of life." I decided to take the path of living. I did not know what David meant about "living." An awesome guy came into my life, became my best friend, and showed me that there was light at the end of the tunnel, regardless of how little I can physically do. David told me, "Just go out and live. Nothing is stopping you, not Muscular Dystrophy, not the power wheelchair but yourself." He was right. I began to "give up everything and let go." I've experienced so many things and perspective that life can offer that I could never in my "old life" have imagined that I would be doing. I decided to take every opportunity that comes my way.

I have always tried to write David Erickson a "thank you" letter but I know a simple "thank you" would never be enough for everything he has done for me and continues to do. He's the hardest person for me to thank because I will never feel that thanking him would be enough. I owe him more than that, my life, for giving me an opportunity of life and not giving up on me that night at the ICU; a "breath of life" as he called it. David put his faith, his whole being and believed in me to be one of those that choose to be strong and live life, and not run away or be selfish or take a cowardly way out and die . . . hence the nickname "Tough Sissy." He never pressured me to get trached or not, but he only offered the road of life to me. Maybe he saw through my heart and felt it wasn't my time to go yet. I may be at a disadvantage in life. I've come this far without giving up. I know he knows people like that won't lose. That's what I want to believe. He gave me his word that everything will be okay.

> "We all struggle to find the right path to take in life. It's not always easy to know what that is or where it will lead us. In the end, it's the people in our lives that provide us the balance to help us make it through." (*Kyle XY*)

Being on the ventilator didn't stop me from living "a breath of life" at Angel View. It's not just for the disabled, but for "opportunities" of life. I was allowed to live life. I continued to do what I never knew would be possible. I go out as much as I can. I get to attend community events: speaking about Angel View, my ventilator, and my life to different types of people, clubs, schools, golf events. I'm enjoying these things that I never knew I could do. I have met so many different types of interesting people. Life did not give up on me; more like life is saying yes. Like a good friend of mine, Raul Pizarro who also has a form of Muscular Dystrophy, would say, "Life Says Yes." It opened its arms and embraced my decisions to not let the challenges of life keep me from living. I'm experiencing life here with a content heart. Life is awesome.

# ABOUT THE AUTHOR

Peter Li is 38 years old, suffers from MD and lives in a wheelchair. Thanks to the incredible work of Angel View, he lives in a home in Southern California and enjoys activities and travel provided by their amazing program. To learn more about Angel View, visit: www.angelview.org.

# Works Cited

*Anais Nin.* GoodReads.com. Web. 2016 <http://www.goodreads.com/work/quotes/1107826-the-diary-of-anas-nin-1931-1934>.

*Anais Nin 2.* GoodReads.com. Web. 2016. <http://www.goodreads.com/quotes/57738-each-contact-with-a-human-being-is-so-rare-so>.

*Anna Robertson Brown Lindsay.* AZQuotes.com. Web. <http://www.azquotes.com/quote/831029>.

*Anonymous, A Friend is One to Whom.* WishAFriend.com. Web. 2016. <http://www.wishafriend.com/quotes/qid/6120/>.

*Anonymous, A True Friend.* Scrapbook.com. Web. 2016. <https://www.scrapbook.com/quotes/doc/16345.html>.

*Anonymous, One of the Hardest Things.* RandomQuotesofLife. Web. 2016. <http://randomquotesoflife-ally.blogspot.com/2011/07/loving-somebody-who-doesnt-love-you.html>.

*Anonymous, There's a Miracle of Friendship.* Scrapbook.com. Web. 2016. <https://www.scrapbook.com/quotes/doc/11630.html>.

*Blue Drop.* Created by Akihito Yoshitomi. Sentai Filmworks, USA. 2007-2008.

*Bluer Than Indigo.* Directed by Masami Shimoda. Funimation. 2002.

*Carl Sandburg.* QuotationsPage.com. Web. <http://www.quotationspage.com/quote/2989.html>.

*Christiane Northrup, M.D.* QuotationsPage.com. Web. 2016. <http://www.quotationspage.com/quote/30987.html>.

*Cindy Lew.* Scrapbook.com. Web. 2016. <https://www.scrapbook.com/quotes/doc/24505.html>.

"Death Be Not Whatever." *Joan of Arcadia.* Written by Barbara Hall, directed by Peter Levin. KCBS. Los Angeles. California. 7 November 2003.

*Demosthenes*. BrainyQuote.com. Xplore Inc, 2016. Web. <https://www.brainyquote.com/quotes/quotes/d/demosthene383346.html>.

Do, Anh. "Decades later, Vietnamese refugees honor Navy commander who rescued them." *Los Angeles Times*. 6 June 2015. Web. <http://www.latimes.com/local/california/la-me-ff-sea-rescue-20150607-story.html>.

*Does It Run in the Family?* April 2000. Web. 17 Feb 2004. <http://www.mdausa.org/publications/fa-dmdbmd-family.html>.

*Eleanor Roosevelt*. QuotationsPage.com. 2016. Web. <http://www.quotationspage.com/quote/2558.html>.

*Facts About Duchenne and Becker Muscular Dystrophies (DMD and BMD)*. n.d. Web. 17 Feb 2004. <https://www.mda.org/disease/duchenne-muscular-dystrophy>.

*Fatal Fury: The Motion Picture*. Written by Yuji Matsumoto and Takashi Yamada, directed by Masami Obari. Studio Cockpit Productions. SNK. Japan. 1994.

*Francis William Bourdillon*. Bartleby.com. Web. 2016. <http://www.bartleby.com/246/979.html>.

*Francois de La Rochefoucauld*. BrainyQuote.com. Xplore Inc, 2016. Web. <https://www.brainyquote.com/quotes/quotes/f/francoisde142634.html>.

*Frederick Buechner*. Values.com. Web. 2016. <http://www.values.com/inspirational-quotes/3166-the-life-i-touch-for-good-or-ill-will-touch>.

"Friday Night." *Joan of Arcadia*. Written by Barbara Hall and Stephen Nathan, directed by Elodie Keene. KCBS. Los Angeles. California.12 November 2004.

*Gloria Steinem*. AllPoetry.com. Web. 2016. <https://allpoetry.com/quote/by/Gloria%20Steinem>.

*Hasidic Saying*. GoodReads.com. Web. 2016. <http://www.goodreads.com/quotes/665783-everyone-should-carefully-observe-which-way-his-heart-draws-him>.

*Henry Bromel*. QuotationsPage.com. Web. <http://www.quotationspage.com/quote/32444.html>.

*Henry Melvill.* Melvilliana. Web. 2016. <http://
melvilliana.blogspot.com/2011/09/finest-thing-herman-
melville-never-said.html>.

*Henry Van Dyke.* PageData.Info. Web. 2016. <https://pagedata.info/
data/4ddb1b6>.

*Ivy Baker Priest.* WisdomQuotes. Web. <http://
www.wisdomquotes.com/quote/ivy-baker-priest.html>.

*The Irresponsible Captain Tylor.* Written by Hitoshi Yoshiyoka,
directed by Koichi Mashimo. Tatsunoko Productions. Tokyo.
1993.

*Keller, Helen.* BrainyQuote.com. Xplore Inc, 2016. Web.<https://
www.brainyquote.com/quotes/quotes/h/
helenkelle101301.html>.

*King Whitney Jr.* QuotationsPage. Web. <http://
www.quotationspage.com/quote/1688.html>.

*Kyle XY.* Created by Eric Bress and Mackye Gruber. Touchstone
Television 2006-2007. ABC Studios. 2007-2009.

Ladner, Joyce A. *Tomorrow's Tomorrow: The Black Woman.*
University of Nebraska Press, 1995. Print.

*Lao Tzu.* BrainyQuote.com. Xplore Inc, 2016. Web. 2016. <https://
www.brainyquote.com/quotes/quotes/l/laotzu118352.html>.

Loreman, Tim. *Love as Pedagogy.* Canada: Sense Publishers, 2011.
Print.

*Madonna.* Goodreads.com. Web. <http://www.goodreads.com/
quotes/123182-to-be-brave-is-to-love-someone-
unconditionally-without-expecting>.

*Mahou Sensei Negima!* Created by Ken Akamatsu, directed by Shin
Onuma. Japan. 2006.

*Major TV.* Written by Takuya, Mitsuda, directed by Kenichi Kasai.
Nippon Housou Kyoukai Productions. Tokyo. 2004.

*Marcel Proust.* BrainyQuote.com. Xplore Inc. Web. 2016. <https://
www.brainyquote.com/quotes/quotes/m/
marcelprou105251.html>.

*Margaret Fairless Barber.* QuotationsBook.comg. Web. <http://
quotationsbook.com/quote/28273/>.

*Margerite Gardiner.* BrainyQuote.com. Xplore Inc. Web. 2016. <https://www.brainyquote.com/quotes/quotes/m/marguerite379090.html>.

*Marisse.* Marisse18.wordpress.com. Web. <https://marisse18.wordpress.com/category/waitinforsomeone/>.

*Martha Beck.* QuotationsPage.com. Web. <http://www.quotationspage.com/quote/31612.html>.

*My Sassy Girl.* Dir. Jae-young Kwak. Perf. Ji-hyun Jun, In-mun Kim Tae-hyun Cha. 2001.

*Naruto Shippûden The Movie: Bonds.* Directed by Hajime Kamegaki. Studio Pierrot. 2008.

"Night Without Stars." *Joan of Arcadia.* Written by Barbara Hall and David Grae, directed by Kevin Dowling.KCBS. Los Angeles, California. 13 February 2004

"Only Connect." *Joan of Arcadia.* Written by Barbara Hall, directed by James Hayman. KCBS. Los Angeles, California. 24 September 2004.

"Our Star, The Leaf Star." *Twin Spica.* Written by Tomomi Mochizuki, directed by Kenshaku Ko. NHK. Tokyo. 31 January 2004.

*Ovid.* Goodreads.com. Web. <http://www.goodreads.com/quotes/412678-love-will-enter-cloaked-in-friendship-s-name>.

*Patricia Russell-McCloud.* CleoEJacksonIII.com. Web. <http://www.cleoejacksoniii.com/my-favorite-quotations.html>.

*Peter Strup.* RheasQuoteBook. Web. <http://rheasquotebook.tumblr.com/post/14930489989/time-only-seems-to-matter-when-its-running-out>.

*Phillip Stanhope, 4th Earl of Chesterfield.* BrainyQuote.com. Xplore Inc, 2016. Web. <https://www.brainyquote.com/quotes/quotes/p/philipstan118711.html>.

"Raisins." *South Park.* Written and directed by Trey Parker. Braniff. 10 December 2003.

*Richard Bach.* GoodReads.com. Web. 2016. <http://www.goodreads.com/quotes/15274-the-bond-that-links-your-true-family-is-not-one>.

"The Rise and Fall of Joan Girardi." *Joan of Arcadia*. Written by Barbara Hall and Lindsay Sturman, directed by Martha Mitchell. KCBS. Los Angeles, California. 28 January 2005.

"Romancing the Joan." *Joan of Arcadia*. Written by Barbara Hall, directed by Joanna Kerns. KCBS. Los Angeles. California. 11 February 2005.

*Rozen Maiden*. Directed by Alexander Von David. Geneon Entertainment. Japan. 7 October 2004.

"Saigo no Shôrisha." *Mobile Suit Gundam Wing*. Directed by Masashi Ikeda. Bandai Entertainment. 2000-2001.

*Sandra Day O'Connor*. WisdomQuotes.com. Web. 2016. <http://www.wisdomquotes.com/quote/sandra-day-oconnor.html>.

*School Days*. Overflow. Directed by Keitaro Motonaga. TNK. Tokyo. 26 May 2006.

Silvestri, Linda. *NCLEX-RN Examination Review*. Canada, 2005. Print.

*Soren Kierkegaard*. BrainyQuote.com. Xplore Inc, 2016. Web. <https://www.brainyquote.com/quotes/quotes/s/sorenkierk105030.html>.

*The Superdimensional Fortress Macross II: Lovers Again*. Written by Tomita Sukehiro, directed *by Kenichi Yantani. Anime International Company. Japan. 21 May 1992.*

*Tennyson, Lord Alfred*. BrainyQuote.com. Xplore Inc, 2015. Web. <https://www.brainyquote.com/quotes/quotes/a/alfredlord153702.html>.

*Terry Lynn Taylor*. QuotationsPage.com. Web. 2016. <http://www.quotationspage.com/quote/30990.html>.

*Thomas á Kempis*. QuotationsPage.com. Web. 2016. <http://www.quotationspage.com/quote/34408.html>.

*Tsubasa Chronicle*. Directed by Koichi Mashimo and Hiroshi Morioka, NHK. 2005.

"The Uncertainty Principle." *Joan of Arcadia*. Written by Joy Gregory, directed by Helen Shaver. KCBS. Los Angeles. California. 12 December 2003.

*Unknown, Time Doesn't Wait.* Pravsworld.com. Web. 2016. <http://www.pravsworld.com/time-doesnt-wait/>.

*Victor Hugo.* Scrapbook.com. Web. 2016. <https://www.scrapbook.com/quotes/doc/30961.html>.

*William Arthur Ward.* GoodReads.com. Web. <https://www.goodreads.com/author/quotes/416931.William_Arthur_Ward>.

*William Jennings Bryan.* GoodReads.com. Web. 2016. <http://www.goodreads.com/quotes/41911-destiny-is-not-a-matter-of-chance-it-is-a>.

"With a little prayer. An oath on the grave." *Yakitate Japan.* Created by Hashiguchi Takashi. Directed by Aoki Yasunao. Sunrise. Tokyo. 22 February 2005.

"Zero wan bakuha shirei." *Mobile Suit Gundam Wing.* Directed by Masashi Ikeda and Shinji Takamatsu. Sunrise. 2000.

Made in the USA
San Bernardino, CA
15 September 2017